Tarot Mysteries

TAROT MYSTERIES

Rediscovering
the
Real Meanings
of the
Cards

JONATHAN DEE

Sterling Publishing Co., Inc.
New York
A Sterling / Zambezi Book

Published by Sterling Publishing Co., Inc.
387 Park Avenue South, New York, NY 10016
Published simultaneously in Great Britain by Zambezi Publishing
Copyright © 2003 Jonathan Dee
Illustrations © 2003 Jonathan Dee

Distributed in Canada by Sterling Publishing
c/o Canadian Manda Group, One Atlantic Avenue, Suite 105
Toronto, Ontario, Canada M6K 3E7
Distributed in Australia by Capricorn Link (Australia) Pty. Ltd.
P.O. Box 704, Windsor, NSW 2756 Australia

ISBN 1-4027-0773-8

This one is for Grant Griffiths;

In making this book a reality, my very close friends Sasha Fenton and Jan Budkowski have both been invaluable, each in their own way; thank you.
May the world turn well for us all.

About the Author

Jonathan Dee has been an astrologer, Tarot card Reader and psychic since the 1970s, having worked all over the United Kingdom and also in the United States. He is well known on radio, television and in a variety of magazines, as a serious historian and folklorist in addition to his other skills.

Jonathan has been the regular daily astrologer for BBC Radio Wales for the past 16 years on a program that is not only the most listened to in Wales but has also received a Sony Award. Besides broadcasting on many other radio and TV channels including BBC Radio 4, Talkradio UK, LBC, HTV, Granada and Carlton both as an astrologer and historian, he has also presented a series of programs for BBC TV exploring the fascinating byways of the history of Wales.

A prolific author, Jonathan has previously partnered with Sasha Fenton in producing the annual Astro-guides series between 1995 and 2000 as well as co-authoring the Moon Sign Kit and *Lucky Day Finder*. Jonathan has also written books on subjects as diverse as illustrated guides to Tarot, Runes, Feng Shui, Color Therapy, Chinese Face Reading and Astrology as well as historical works on Ancient Egypt and the history of Prophecies.

Many of Jonathan Dee's books have been translated into languages as diverse as Portuguese, Spanish, Finnish, Greek and Japanese.

Jonathan lives in Cardiff, Wales, with a cute mongrel named Tazmania, and no one is more amazed at the way things turn out than he is.

Contents

1

The Mystery of the Tarot Cards

This book is about Tarot cards, as indeed are many others. What makes this one different is that it does not just give instructions on how to read the cards, or concentrate solely on the 22 picture cards that are regarded as being particularly special. On the contrary, I hope to have given a balanced and informative perspective on each of the cards, as well as an overview of the entire deck.

This is not just a book about reading the cards, but about why the cards *are* the cards, why each picture forms part of a particular sequence and why the Tarot occupies the mystical place that it does in our consciousness. The biggest question is yet to come, and that is: "Why do the individual cards have their own particular meanings?" The answers to all these questions will lead us down some strange and obscure byways into areas as diverse as Celtic mythology, Hebrew mysticism, Renaissance theatrical productions and the stars and planets of astrology.

First, let us tackle what a deck of Tarot cards actually is. There are 78 cards in a classical Tarot deck, but the first complication arises because the Tarot is not one deck, but two. These two parts are called the Major Arcana, comprising 22 cards, and the Minor Arcana of 56 cards. The word Arcana is Latin in origin and means "secret," so if you were pedantic, you could describe each individual card as an "Arcanum."

The 22 Major cards each have a symbolic picture on them, and are also described as "Trumps" or "Atu." This is a word that is said to be Ancient Egyptian for "key," but in fact is more likely to have derived from the French "A tout"—literally, "to all." This also means "a key," in the sense that it opens the door to the whole of the subject—or even to everything in heaven and earth. To clinch matters, the word "atout" means "trumps," which is apt as this also refers to the Major Arcana cards.

The 56 cards of the Minor Arcana are more familiar. They are divided into four suits that are usually called Wands, Coins, Cups and Swords. These have evolved into the modern pack of playing cards with Wands becoming Clubs, Coins becoming Diamonds, Cups becoming Hearts and Swords becoming Spades. Like the modern deck, the Minor cards have kings, queens and knaves, but they also possess four extra cards, which are the knights of each suit.

These enigmatic cards have been used for the purposes of divination since at least 1500 A.D. The reason for their survival is that they work. After all, we abandoned other practices such as gazing into the entrails of chickens because they did not work—and because such tools were less portable and convenient than a deck of cards. The act of shuffling and dealing the cards is a potent symbol of the workings of fate. The hand of cards you receive isn't yours to choose, but how you play them...well, that's up to you.

When I began the research for this book, I did so with the confidence of having written two previous guides on how to read and interpret the cards. However, as I carried on, I quickly became amazed at how little I actually knew. I shouldn't have been—after all, Tarot cards have been a feature of Western culture for at least six hundred years. A lot can change in that time—and does! What is accepted truth in one era is errant falsehood in the next. Fashions in all things change like the wind when looked at in hindsight.

Of course, not everyone will agree with every aspect of this book and some might be inclined to quibble over this or that historical snippet. Others will have a different view of the more mystical or astrological interpretations, but even so, if this book leads to a realization that there is more to the Tarot than one suspects, then it will have done its job.

Researching and writing this book has been a revelation to me; I hope that reading it will be a revelation to you.

Jonathan Dee, Cardiff, Wales

January 2003

2

The History of the Tarot

At the outset, I have to say that writing a complete and definitive history of the Tarot cards is impossible to achieve. For a start, we do not know who invented them, who devised their intricate symbolism, or indeed, who popularized them as a form of entertainment, either for card games or for the purposes of fortune telling. However, it is wrong to assume that nothing whatsoever can be revealed about the cards' origins or the uses to which they were put, even if there is no convenient documentary evidence. In short, the history of Tarot cards is not a matter of studying precise, coherent records, but of putting small snippets of information together to try to arrive at a solution to the puzzle.

Many previous writers have come up with their own theories, and indeed some wild speculations about the cards and what they mean. For example, one of the earliest theorists, Antoine de Court de Gebelin (1719–1784) had no hesitation in firmly avowing that the Tarot was undoubtedly of Ancient Egyptian origin. In his time no one had yet deciphered hieroglyphics, and furthermore it was very fashionable to ascribe anything that was in any way mysterious to the land of the Nile. A further elaboration of his claims was that the Gypsies had introduced the Tarot to Europe and that they were a pictorial form of a branch of Jewish mysticism based on the Hebrew alphabet known as the Qabalah. (The precise spelling seems to be uncertain, because this word also occurs as Kabbalah, Cabala, Cabballah and so on.)

De Gebelin's ideas were taken up with enthusiasm by early 19th century French occultists, most notably a Parisian wig maker called Alliette (1738–1791), who also made a side living as a fortuneteller. Alliette (he later reversed his name to become Etteilla) claimed to have been educated by the great Count St. Germain himself. Apart from being an occult adept and an accomplished tanner by trade, the stylish and plausible St. Germain also implied that he was an immortal and that he had known Cleopatra and Christ intimately.

By far the most intellectually profound of the French mystics was Alphonse Louis Constant (1810–1875), who, after translating his name into Hebrew, became known as Eliphas Levi. Levi created a method of incorporating both the Qabalah and astrology into the symbolism of the Tarot cards. Indeed it is his methodology that is still followed by the Tarot readers of France and southern Europe.

Occultists of Northern Europe took a different route, a path that was begun by yet another extraordinary eccentric named Samuel Liddell MacGregor Mathers (1854–1918). After years of research into alchemy, astrology and other related subjects in the library of the British Museum, Mathers became convinced that although Levi had been on the right track, he had nevertheless got it wrong. To prove the point, Mathers created his own system of attributions combining numerology, Qabalah and astrology. It was this system he taught to his followers in an upper class mystical society that he jointly founded, which rejoiced in the high-flown title of the Hermetic Order of the Golden Dawn. Consequently, Mathers' theories are now known as the Golden Dawn system of attributions, and in the main, these have been followed throughout this book.

There were two further significant Tarot developments, both of which were instigated by Golden Dawn members. The first was the creation of a fully illustrated Tarot deck by Arthur Edward Waite (1857–1942) with the assistance of Pamela Coleman Smith (d 1951). This was published in 1909. The second development was an elaboration of the Mathers method that culminated in the creation of the Thoth Tarot deck, illustrated by Lady Frieda Harris (1877–1962). This latter deck was the brainchild of a former pupil of Mathers, who, with characteristic modesty, regarded himself as superior to all other occult thinkers living or dead. This was, of course, the man who relished describing himself as "The Great Beast," Aleister Crowley (1875–1947).

Without being judgmental in any way, I have endeavored to include the views of de Gebelin, Levi, Mathers, Waite and Crowley, in addition to those of more modern commentators, without too much unnecessary comment as to their relative merits.

The Known Facts

When all is said and done, all the ideas and speculations (worthy or otherwise) put forward by the notable occult intellectuals since the eighteenth century add nothing to our knowledge of the true origin of the cards. What we do know is that, at some time during the first half of the fifteenth century (between 1420 and 1440), probably in Northern Italy, somebody devised the first recognizable set of 78 cards that we would call Tarot. There is no evidence whatsoever that the 22 cards of the Major Arcana originated in any other time or in any other place.

It was long believed that a certain alchemist called Jacques Gringonneur invented the cards to amuse his king, the mad Charles VI of France in 1392, because it was recorded that he was paid to paint three decks by the royal accountant. Sixteen of the surviving Major Arcana cards and one Minor card are kept in the Bibliotheque National in Paris. These are called the "Charles VI" deck. However, the style of these cards suggests that they actually come from Northern Italy and were painted about a century after Gringonneur completed his commission. It is therefore likely that the cards that Jacques Gringonneur presented to his monarch were a set of Minor Arcana cards.

The 56 "small" cards apparently already existed, and they were familiar to gamblers and probably to fortunetellers as well. The Minor Arcana cards had existed for at least a century and had a mystery and symbolism all of their own (see the section in this book on the Four Grail Hallows). The Minor cards with their four suits are still in daily use, having evolved into the familiar modern playing card deck.

The addition of 22 "special" cards then known as "Trionfi" or Triumphs, which did not belong to any suit, mark the Tarot as being unusual to say the least. These Triumphs, which we now know as "Trumps," were used in a game similar to Bridge, where they outranked all other cards. This was the game of Triumphs, which caught on amongst the upper classes, initially in Italy and France, later spreading to Sicily, Austria and the German states as far north as the Netherlands. The lower classes may also have used the cards, but the pastimes of the ordinary folk were not regarded as being important and therefore tended to go unrecorded. What we are left with are various vague, incomplete references, usually from monkish sources.

The very first reference to cards of any sort was, unsurprisingly, written by a monk named Johannes of Brefeld in the middle of the 1300s. Johannes said that the game of cards had images of kings and knights, and was played far too often for the piety of the people. However, in 1377, Johannes Von Rheinfelden of Switzerland wrote that playing cards describe the state of the world and are valuable tools for the education of morals.

In 1450 the Duke of Milan, Francesco Sforza, wrote a letter in which he specifically mentions both triumph cards and playing cards, clearly distinguishing between them. Duke Francesco purchased one of the surviving early Tarot decks that had been painted by Bonifacio Bembo. This is significant, because the Sforza family figures in a compelling theory of the origins of the cards that is given at the end of this chapter.

During the Congress of Mantua in 1459, a strange deck of cards was made for no less a personage than Pope Pius II and two cardinals, for a pastime called "the Game of the Governance of the World." These cards have been ascribed to the Renaissance artist Andrea Mantegna. However, although these are regarded as a Tarot deck, they are not the deck with which we are familiar. They comprised 50 symbolic cards that were divided into ranks; many of the images are very similar to those found in the classic Tarot deck.

The first of these ranks is called the "Estates of Man." The lowest card is the Beggar, which is very similar to the Fool, there follows the Servant, the Artisan (the Magician), the Merchant, the Gentleman, the Knight, the Duke, the King, the Emperor and the Pope. The latter two are indistinguishable from conventional Tarot designs of the period, while the Servant and the King resemble their equivalents in the Minor Arcana. The Knight, however, bears no similarity to other Tarot knights.

The rank above humanity consists of classical images of the nine Muses, goddesses of inspiration and Apollo, who was the god of poetry and prophecy. Above them are images representing the liberal arts and sciences. These are Grammar, Logic, Rhetoric, Geometry, Arithmetic, Music, Astrology, Poetry, Philosophy and Theology. There follow the Christian Virtues of Faith, Hope and Charity and the so-called Classical Virtues of Strength, Justice, Temperance and Prudence, together with the spirits of the Sun, the Cosmos and Time. Some of these images are also found in the conventional Tarot deck. The final and highest rank is that of the Celestial Spheres, with the seven planets, the Stars, the Prime Mover (or moment of creation) and the First Cause, God himself.

Cardinal Nicholas of Cusa wrote of the Mantegna cards: "This game is not played in a childish way, but as the Holy Wisdom played it for God at the beginning of the World." By 1482, attitudes to the cards were somewhat less spiritual, because the less than aptly named Lorenzo Spirito wrote a book on fortune telling based on 20 questions arranged around a wheel of fortune. Lorenzo refers to 20 "kings" or major cards and the use of a dice, which can give 56 answers. It may be significant that 56 is the number of cards in the Minor Arcana.

Other books on fortune telling appeared in Mainz and Basle in 1510, while the poet Pietro Aretino (1492–1556) in his "Dialogues" (1525) makes many references to the Tarot. One special reference is that "They reveal the secrets of nature, the reason for things, and explain the causes why day is driven out by night and night by day."

The Cards and the Cosmos

Both Cardinal Nicholas of Cusa and Pietro Aretino were of the opinion that the cards explained things. It is certain that Nicholas of Cusa thought of the Mantegna cards as a kind of map of the universe and of man's place within it, and this manner of symbolic logic can be applied to the Tarot.

It has been pointed out that each of the Major cards when taken in turn can symbolically "trump" or triumph over the card that precedes it. So if we begin with the Fool, then folly is trumped by knowledge symbolized by the Magician or Juggler. In turn, knowledge is trumped by wisdom (the Priestess), however her cold virginity is no match for the fertility of the Empress. The female power of the Empress is defeated by the (admittedly a sexist view) masculinity of the Emperor, whose worldly power must bow before the spiritual authority of the Pope or Hierophant. Even his faith cannot stand in the way of love (the Lovers), but war, symbolized by the Chariot, can part even the most devoted couple. The conquering hero of the Chariot can likewise be overcome by Strength, and even Strength may fade with time at the onset of old age shown as the Hermit. Yet young or old, strong or weak, wise or foolish, all on this earth are under the sway of the Wheel of Fortune. This sequence of cards completes the "earthly" part of the Tarot.

All of the above might have been found in the pious Mantegna Tarot, which would have earned the approval of Nicholas of Cusa. However, now the cards take a darker turn and instead of ascending ever upward to the divine, the next "rank" leads us firstly into the depths of hell, only then to rise into the celestial regions of heaven.

The story is taken up again with the divine Justice, which is above the vagaries of Fortune. However, Justice has a harsh side and can condemn to punishment for crimes, as shown by the Hanged Man. The result of his predicament is usually Death, but even Death can be overcome by divine mercy, as shown by

Temperance. However, even Temperance can be lured into temptation by the wiles of the Devil. But the Devil himself once fell from Heaven, even as Nimrod did from his Tower, so he is no longer among the Stars. The brilliance of the Stars is outshone by that of the Moon, which in turn is outshone by the glory of the Sun. Yet even the Sun's splendor is nothing as compared to the wonder of the glorious day of resurrection shown by Judgement or the Angel.

Now we arrive at the problem with this way of looking at the Trump cards. If this sequence is correct, then what trumps the Angel? Does the World card represent God? After all God is at the very top of the tree, so to speak, so does the highest card represent the All Highest? If so, then this is neither the God of Abraham nor the wise old man seated on a cloud in glory that is such a common image. Instead, a naked young woman dances within a victory wreath, surrounded by symbolic images representing the four directions, the four fixed signs of the zodiac, the four elements, the four seasons and endless other symbolic fours. However, in a sermon delivered at some time toward the end of the fifteenth century, this view seems to be endorsed by a certain Reverend Steele, who referred to the card as "The World, that is, God the Father."

It has been suggested that this figure represents an embryo, that the end of the sequence is also the beginning, because after the embryo comes the child, and the child is the Fool and that brings us back to the start again. On the other hand, the dancing girl may show a soul in paradise, or make the symbolic statement that the sequence of the cards is the way the world is!

The Order of the Game of Trionfi

(N.B: These rules are a basic outline; the Fool, for example, can be a wild card like our present day Joker).

- A Major card is trumped by the Fool, which, when it represents folly, is trumped by the Magician.
- The Magician denotes knowledge, but it is trumped by the High Priestess.
- The High Priestess symbolizes wisdom and Purity, but she is trumped by the Empress.
- The Empress is associated with fertility and femininity, but she is trumped by the Emperor.
- The Emperor stands for worldly power and masculinity, but he is trumped by the Hierophant or Pope.
- The Hierophant or Pope represents faith and spiritual authority, but he is trumped by the Lovers.
- The Lovers are associated with love and physical passions, but they are trumped by the Chariot.
- The Chariot signifies war but is trumped by Strength.
- Strength represents victory and vigor, but he is trumped by the Hermit.
- The Hermit signals time and old age, but he is trumped by the Wheel of Fortune.
- The Wheel of Fortune stands for fortune, but this is trumped by Justice.
- Justice denotes mercy and severity, but she is trumped by the Hanged Man.
- The Hanged Man symbolizes punishment, but he is trumped by Death.
- Death is trumped by Temperance.
- Temperance indicates mercy and right living, but she is trumped by the Devil.
- The Devil represents temptation, but he is trumped by the Tower.
- The Tower tells of pride, but this is trumped by the Star.
- The Star stands for hope, but this is trumped by the Moon.

- The Moon indicates mystery, but she is trumped by the Sun.
- The Sun symbolizes clarity, but he is trumped by Judgement.
- Judgement represents resurrection, but this is trumped by the World.
- The World signifies God, paradise, the womb, but it is trumped by the Fool.

This starts the sequence again.

In my view, this is a perfectly sensible way of looking at the sequence of Major Arcana cards. Again, if I may venture an opinion, despite the elaborations of the symbolism of the cards in later centuries, this is probably the way an educated person would have viewed the cards in the fifteenth and sixteenth centuries. It was the style of those times to delight in puzzles, hidden messages and layer upon layer of secret meanings. Therefore, one may conclude that the obvious numerical sequence is not the only way in which to reveal the symbolism of the cards. Even the pious Nicholas of Cusa would have recognized this arrangement of the cards in ranks:

The Earthly World	**The Estates of Man**
the Fool	Beggar or folly
The Magician	Artisan or knowledge
The Empress	Fertility
The Emperor	Worldly power
The High Priestess	Intuitive wisdom
The Pope	Religion and faith
The Fates or Lovers	Love
The Chariot	War
The Hermit	Time
The Wheel of Fortune	Fortune
The Virtues	
Strength	
Justice	
Temperance	

Hell
The Hanged Man
Death
The Devil
The Tower
Heaven
The Star
The Moon
The Sun
The World (God)

The Visconti Triumph

One very compelling theory concerning the origin of the Major Arcana was put forward, not by an occultist or a playing card historian, but by a librarian. Her name was Gertrude Moakley and her enthusiasm was for cataloging. As a research tool and a trial for her new system, she decided to use the cards painted by Bembo as a test subject. No one had systematically analyzed the early Tarot before. Moakley was soon fascinated by her findings and she published them in 1966. In her version of events, Gertrude Moakley begins by asking the reader to imagine the scene in fifteenth-century Milan, during a carnival procession in the presence of the illustrious Duke of the city, Francesco Sforza, and his wife the Duchess Bianca Maria Visconti.

The first to take the stage is the Carnival King, a fast-talking master of ceremonies with magic tricks and capacity for word play. In the tradition of the time, he would be dressed in red and would preside over the parade until his mock execution at the end of the performance, which will coincide with the beginning of Lent. His companion, a ragged clown, has no fixed place in the procession but seems to pop up everywhere as a reminder that the frivolity of carnival will end soon. Moakley implies that this character in his poverty is symbolic of the penitence of Lent itself.

Then the parade floats arrive with a triumphal chariot bearing Cupid, who directs his arrow at a pair of Lovers who are dressed to represent the Duke and Duchess. Other captives of Cupid are the Emperor and Empress, the Pope and Papess (a scandalous episode in the history of Milan's ruling dynasty occurred when Manfreda Visconti was actually elected Pope by a heretical sect. The inclusion of a figure representing Manfreda in the carnival would have been a daring act).

The procession continues with Temperance and Fortitude (this being a play on the Duke's surname, Sforza) and a great wheel representing Fortune. Footmen attend carrying staves, cups, swords and coins. Next the grinning figure of ghastly Death dances into view accompanied by Time and the Devil. The Tower symbolizes Pride, but the Hanged Man who appears as an acrobat on a gallows follows this. This is another daring inclusion, because the Duke's father had been condemned to die as a traitor to the Pope.

The final tableau is the triumph of eternity, so here is Justice, the Sun, the Moon, the Stars and a glorious depiction of the Four Holy Living Creatures who surround the throne of God. Yet, as a witty twist, a dancing girl expresses the joy of living, while angels loudly blow their trumpets to the applause of the crowd.

At the end of the carnival, its mock king suffers an equally mock execution, a bonfire of the vanities is built, into which the Fool invites the people to throw their playing cards and other symbols of idle pleasure as a gesture of repentance.

Gertrude Moakley's ideas are interesting, but they do not constitute any proof. There is no record of a procession such as this, even though this was the right era for such an extravaganza. Much less for a deck of cards painted to commemorate the occasion. In the end, as compelling as this theory is, we are back to a speculation as ornate as that of Court de Gebelin, Levi, Mathers, Crowley and the rest.

The true origins of the Tarot remain a mystery, but it is a mystery with clues, these being found in the images of the cards themselves, and the occult themes that underlie them. Most notably, these are the signs and planets of astrology, and the complexities of the Holy Qabalah.

3

The Holy Qabalah

Although the Tarot has been influenced by many occult theories in its history, it has no greater affinity than with the Holy Qabalah. The Qabalah (often spelled in a number of ways including Cabala, Caballa, Kaballah, Quabalah and many other variations) is originally a symbolic Hebrew mystical system based on a complex form of numerology allied to the 22 letters of the Hebrew alphabet and a diagram known as the Tree of Life. This esoteric system is held to be the very blueprint of creation, explaining the nature of the physical and spiritual universe. The Qabalah has been a powerful influence on western occultism since at least the Middle Ages, and many Tarot theorists, including Alliette, Levi, Mathers and Crowley were convinced that it provides the foundation of the cards themselves.

The Mythical Beginnings of the Qabalah

Some of the oldest traditions of Jewish thought give a mythological slant to the origins of the Qabalah. Medieval rabbis claimed that the mysteries of the Qabalah were revealed to the prophet Moses when he encountered the Divine in the form of the Burning Bush on Mount Sinai. The outward sign of this divine revelation were the Ten Commandments. The inner, secret doctrine was none other than the Qabalah itself.

An alternative view gives us yet another link to ancient Egypt. According to the Biblical Book of Exodus, Moses was discovered in a basket or "ark" in the reeds of the Nile by Pharaoh's daughter, who then raised him as her own son. He grew up as a prince of Egypt, and so the theory goes, was privy to the occult secrets enshrined in the great temples of that evocative civilization. It is in these temples that Moses learned the secrets of the universe and also to master them, becoming a mighty magician. So Qabalistic magic lay behind the Ten Plagues of Egypt, the transformation of staves into snakes, the creation of a spring in the desert, the parting of the Red Sea and all the other wonders that Moses performed on behalf of the Hebrew people. Of course, all these feats were performed in accordance with the will of his God.

This version of the story suggests an intriguing possibility that the God of Moses, far from originally being a tribal deity of fire and war as is hinted at by the revelation of the Burning Bush, is to be identified with the supreme Egyptian god Amun or Ammon. The very name of this god means "the Unseen One" and as we all know, it is forbidden in Jewish tradition to portray God in pictorial form. Amun was also said to have a secret name, a word of such power that it brought the universe into being. Likewise, following Moses, the name of the God of the Old Testament was not to be spoken aloud or even written down. As a final point, Amun's totem beast was the ram, and there is a persistent tradition that Moses himself possessed horns, as is shown in Michelangelo's statue in St. Peter's in Rome.

Another perspective of the identity of the Hebrew God was favored by no less a figure than Sigmund Freud, the "father" of psychoanalysis. Freud was of the opinion that Judaism itself was an offshoot of the heretical breakaway religion of the Pharaoh, Akhnaten (1352 to 1336 B.C.). Some have gone further and identified this Pharaoh with Moses himself. However, the main point of the argument is that the deity of this new religion was the visible sun disc known as the Aten. It is true that one of the Jewish names for God is Adonai, meaning "The Lord." The word Adonai is derived from the Egyptian Aten.

It is said that the fabled wisdom of King Solomon was also derived from the mysteries of the Qabalah. Indeed, by the Middle Ages, the traditions of three faiths, Jewish, Christian and Islamic, were in agreement that Solomon had been a master magician with the ability to understand the language of the birds and to imprison unruly spirits in bottles. He was also said to have authored several "grimoires" or books of magic such as the "Clavicle of Solomon." Needless to say the spells and talismans in these works were based on Qabalistic principles.

Long after the time of Moses and Solomon, a group of learned rabbis met to create a form of secret society in which the doctrines of the Qabalah could be discussed, taught to new initiates and, most importantly, applied to influence the history of mankind. Indeed, it has been a tradition that the Qabalah is only taught to rabbis and forms an inner doctrine of Judaism too obscure and disturbing for the mass of the populace.

The Elders of Zion?

This version of Qabalistic origins may have inadvertently given rise to a pernicious streak of anti-Semitism by proposing that the world is secretly controlled by a hidden school of Jewish mystics to whom it has been easy to ascribe sinister motives. The most infamous example of this ridiculous idea emerged in the late nineteenth century in a document entitled "The Protocols of the Elders of Zion." A venomous work of fiction, originating in Russia, purporting to reveal the fiendish plans of this secret society to subvert and eventually overthrow Christendom and dominate the world. Although the protocols have been known to be spurious since 1921, they have nevertheless been used to promote and excuse prejudices against the Jewish people and faith throughout the following century. But enough of mythology, both Qabalistic and anti-Semitic, as we move on to what is actually known about the origins of the Qabalah.

The Book of Formation

There are two works that are central to Qabalistic thought. The first of these is called the "Sepher Yetzirah" or "The Book of Formation." This book was written at some time before the sixth century A.D. The Book of Formation is less than two thousand words long and is thought to have been composed by an enlightened Jewish mystic named Rabbi Akiba (or Akiva) who lived around the turn of the first century A.D. Rabbi Akiba was originally a shepherd whose teachings won a reputation for holiness and wisdom. He became a revered Jewish leader, but was involved in an uprising against the Roman rulers and was executed in 138 A.D. Be that as it may, the Book of Formation stresses the importance of the 22 letters of the Hebrew alphabet, claiming that they provide the key to understanding the mysteries of creation and of the universe itself. Twelve of the letters are connected with the signs of the zodiac, the months of the year, twelve organs of the body and twelve senses and functions of man. These functions are sight, hearing, smell, taste, sex, work, movement, anger, humor, imagination and finally sleep.

A further seven letters relate to the classical planets, the days of the week and also the seven directions, (north, south, east west, above, below and center). In human terms, these seven letters relate to the seven openings of the head, the two nostrils, two eyes, two ears and the mouth. The remaining three, Aleph, Mem, Shin are called "mother letters" and are symbolically connected to three of the four classical elements, in this case Air, Fire and Water.

Many scholars hold the opinion that if Rabbi Akiba did indeed write the Book of Formation, he did not make it all up, but that he recorded far more ancient mystical beliefs. Beliefs which held that everything in the universe is made of numbers and letters, and can be understood in terms of this classification. This is the reason that in Jewish tradition, the name of God may not be written down. To do so would be to reveal the letters of the name and the writer could gain understanding of the nature and powers of God, in some sense "stealing" some of that inexpressible power. It is known that the name itself is comprised of four letters so a common way of referring to it was as the "Tetragrammaton" or "The Four-Lettered Word." The Jewish people went to great lengths to come up with euphemisms for the sacred name, many of which are familiar today, such as "The Almighty," "The Lord," "The Lord of Hosts" and many others. It is also of interest to note that in Ancient Egyptian mythology, the goddess Isis gained her mighty magical powers by tricking her grandfather, the sun god Ra, into telling her his true, hidden name. Furthermore, by the eighteenth Dynasty, Ra had become identified with the mysterious Amun as well as becoming briefly transformed into the Aten.

Gematria

Hebrew letters also serve as numerical values, so it is easy to see that to the ancient rabbis, words whose values added up to the same number, must in some mystical sense have a relationship to each other. The art of understanding these relationships is called Gematria.

To simply demonstrate this art, let us take a common word such as "love." In Hebrew, this translates to AHBH (Hebrew has no written vowels).

If we refer to the table of letters and numbers (below), we find that:

A (aleph) = 1
H (he)　　 = 5 and is used twice
B (beth)　 = 2
Therefore the word AHBH adds up to 13.

This is also the sum of the word AChD (aleph = 1, cheth = 8, daleth = 4, adding up to 13), meaning unity, so there is a relationship between love and unity.

It is obvious that Gematria became the basis of the Qabalistic branch of numerology.

Hebrew Letter	Numerical Value
Aleph	1
Beth	2
Gimel	3
Daleth	4
He	5
Vau	6
Zain	7
Cheth	8
Teth	9
Yod	10
Kaph	20
Lamed	30
Mem	40
Nun	50
Samekh	60
Ayin	70
Pe	80
Tzaddi	90
Qoph	100
Resh	200
Shin	300
Tau	400

Of course, to the devout rabbis, the only proper use for Gematria was to discover the hidden meanings of phrases in the divinely inspired Bible itself. So when the statement is made in the Book of Genesis that Abraham was on the plains of Mamre "...and lo three men stood by him." The phrase "...and lo three men" in the original Hebrew adds to 701. A thirteenth-century Qabalist named Eleazar of Worms diligently worked out that the words, "These were Michael, Gabriel and Raphael," also adds up to 701. Thus a new level of understanding was given to the experience of the patriarch Abraham on the plains of Mamre.

Before we leave the subject of the letters themselves and their use in the art of Gematria, the question of their symbolic origin should be addressed. It would be reasonable to assume (as many have) that, if the whole of the Qabalah is Egyptian in origin, then the symbolism of the letters should bear some relation to ancient Egyptian hieroglyphs. When the young French scholar Champolion finally deciphered hieroglyphics in the early part of the nineteenth century (an art that had been lost for nearly two thousand years), he discovered that many hieroglyphic symbols did indeed form an alphabet, the letter A being represented by a vulture, D by a hand and so on. The Hebrew alphabet also has images associated with it, but these seem to bear little relation to their Egyptian counterparts. In the case of Hebrew, A is symbolized by an ox rather than a vulture, D by a door rather than by a hand.

The Book of Splendor

The second seminal Qabalistic work is the "Zohar" or "The Book of Splendor." It is also thought that a pupil of Rabbi Akiba named Rabbi Simon ben Jochai had written this in the first century A.D. In the Zohar, the principle of inter-connection is the primary doctrine. The central theme is that everything in the universe has an affinity with everything else and that every part of creation is involved in a subtle interaction with every other part. This underlying complexity is best expressed in the diagram of the Tree of Life.

Following the Zohar, the Qabalah disappeared from history until it resurfaced in thirteenth century Spain. This renewed interest was spurred on by a new Qabalistic work called "Sepher Bahir" or "The Book of Brilliance," which proposed a picture of the universe as a vast, multifaceted intersection of planes of existence, which lay beneath our mundane reality. This work was followed by such notable figures as Moses de Leon, who brought out his own version of the Zohar, and Abraham Abulafia, who practiced Qabalistic breathing techniques and body postures that we would find akin to the eastern disciplines of yoga.

The expulsion of the Moors and the subsequent flight or forced conversion of the Jews from Spain after 1492 coincided with the expansion of the printing process in Europe. The strong desire of many European princes to throw off the shackles of a repressive church led intellectuals to embrace the newly available non-Christian sources of knowledge. The same movement that brought the works of Plato and Socrates to northern Europe also brought the Qabalah to a much wider audience.

It is an irony of history that the same process that revealed this strand of Jewish mystical thought to Christian Europe also opened the door to other philosophies and other examples of "pagan" literature, most especially the "Hermetica." This was a group of writings composed in Alexandria in the latter part of the Roman Empire, dealing primarily with alchemy, astrology and magic. From the point of view of the mystically inclined intellectuals of Europe, the Qabalah and the Hermetic writings became interchangeable and indeed, though their origins differed, they were seen to be two aspects of the same thing. From this point in time, there were two separate Qabalistic traditions. The Jewish form, eventually leading to the formation of the Hasidic branch of that religion, and the "Christian," or to be more accurate, the "Hermetic Qabalah" of Renaissance thinkers. It is this latter branch with its multitude of associations to astrology, pagan deities, alchemy, ceremonial magic, numerology and symbolism that came to influence the development of Tarot cards.

The Qabalistic Universe

Although the basic principles of the Qabalah are relatively easy to grasp, the totality of the system is so complex that almost anything said about it is bound to be an oversimplification. Be that as it may, the mystical traditions of this extraordinary system begin with the concept of God. In Qabalistic terms, this deity is called "Ain Soph" or "the Boundless." There can be no limits placed on this being, because it encompasses everything. It cannot be described as a "He," as in conventional religion, because if Ain

Soph is to be classified as male, then it could not encompass female. Likewise, and this part is difficult, Ain Soph cannot even be said to exist, because to exist precludes non-existence, and Ain Soph is beyond all such definitions and paradoxes.

From Ain Soph come the ten spheres of the Tree of Life, in descending order from Kether the Crown; the first mover, or first created; eventually to Malkuth, the Kingdom, the physical universe. This act of creation can be imagined as a series of ten cups or glasses, an indefinable "something" that we can imagine as a liquid, but which actually represents the divine will or urge to create, poured from the Ain Soph to fill the topmost of these containers. This topmost cup is Kether. When Kether was full it overflowed into the next, lower cup Chockmah, which in turn filled to overflow into the next, Binah. This created the topmost triangle of the tree, these three being known as the "Supernals." These three spheres continued to overflow, creating three more containers called Geburah, Hesed and Tiphareth and these in turn filled three more, Hod, Netzah and Yesod. Finally the remnants of the divine "liquid" reached the material plane to create the physical universe as symbolized by the tenth sphere, Malkuth.

Another way of imagining this process is to think of God as a great light. This light is shone into a mirror, which then reflects it into another, and this into yet another, until the light has been bounced back and forth ten times. With each reflection the light loses something of its original intensity, until finally only a dim glimmer of the divine can be seen in our corrupt material world.

In Hebrew, these are containers or mirrors of the divine. They are usually thought of as spheres and are called "Sephira" (plural: Sephirot), a word literally meaning "number," and indeed, each sphere is given a number from one to ten, plus a name. The manner in which the creative force flowed described the "Pathways" of the Tree of Life. These are 22 in number, and a letter of the Hebrew alphabet is allocated to each pathway, as well as a numerical value and numerous symbolic associations. But before we go on to examine the pathways in detail, a little more time should be spent

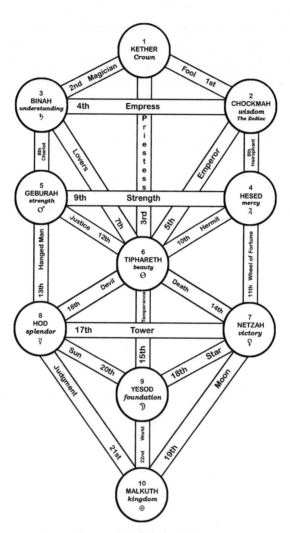

The Tree of Life

with the profound implications of the ten Sephirot and the structure of the Tree of Life itself.

If the ten spheres of the Tree of Life are divided horizontally into groups, they can be imagined as three separate triangles.

The uppermost, consisting of Kether, Chockmah and Binah, points towards the infinite and is called the Supernal triangle.

Below that is the ethical triangle containing Chesed, Geburah and Tiphareth, and at the bottom of the Tree is the astral triangle, which includes Netzah, Hod and Malkuth.

The spheres may also be viewed vertically as three "pillars." The three spheres (Binah, Geburah and Hod) on the left of the diagram make up the "Pillar of Severity," and the three on the right (Chockmah, Chesed and Netzah) have the name "Pillar of Mercy."

These pillars have survived under the names Jakin and Boaz in Masonic tradition, as well as turning up in various guises in the Major Arcana of the Tarot deck.

Between these two extremes lies the "Pillar of Mildness" (Kether, Tiphareth, Yesod and Malkuth) showing the middle way between them.

The First Sphere—Kether the Crown

Kether is the first of the Sephirot and thus the closest to the infinite. Of this Sephira it is said, "It is the Divine Glory, that Light which surpasseth the glory of the Sun and beside which the light of mortals is but darkness, and concerning which it is not fitting that we should speak more fully." Indeed it would be difficult to speak of Kether more fully because its brilliance is such that it is, like the Ain Soph, beyond human understanding. Kether is considered to be "the Prime Mover," the first, created before creation as symbolized in the words of the Biblical Book of Genesis, "Let there be light, and there was light." It has been suggested that William Blake's painting "The Ancient of Days" expresses the concept of the ordering of the universe associated with Kether the Crown. Indeed, the magical image for this Sephira is that of an old, bearded man seen in profile, one side of his face visible and the other not. This

Sephira may also be related to the Native American concept of the Great Spirit. In traditional Qabalistic belief, the soul that reaches this, the highest point of the tree, achieves union with God.

The Second Sphere—Chockmah, Wisdom

The first emanation of Kether is Chockmah, a word that means wisdom. Chockmah is the ultimate male principle and therefore part of the primal duality. In Chinese terms, Chockmah would be described as absolute Yang, being light, dynamic and positive. The familiar image of God as an old, wise man sitting enthroned on a cloud would fit the concept of Chockmah perfectly, as indeed would any father-god from any religion one could possibly name. Here is the perfect image of Zeus, Jupiter, Odin the All-Father, The August Personage of Jade, the Celtic Dagda and all the rest. Chockmah is called "The Father of Fathers" and symbolizes the cause of all activity, growth and movement.

The vision of the prophet Ezekiel speaks of the angels of this Sephira as mighty wheels having "the spirit of life in them." Another way of putting this would be "the spirit of God." As we shall see, this spirit of God came upon the waters of the next Sephira, Binah. The symbolism of Chockmah is phallic in nature; the rod, the tower and the straight line connecting two points. In astrological terms, the second sphere, the circle of the zodiac represents Chockmah, or to be more correct, the entire starry sky.

The Third Sphere—Binah, Understanding

The balance to Chockmah is found in Binah, the second emanation. As Chockmah is wisdom and the male principle, so Binah is understanding and the female half of the great duality. This is the primal Yin, the feminine, dark, receptive side to the equation. Binah is imagined as a great sea, an ocean of understanding. This is the very sea that the spirit of God (as symbolized by Chockmah) came upon to begin creation. As Chockmah is active wisdom, so Binah is depth of comprehension and the compassion that goes with it.

The image of Binah is of the Great Goddesses of the world's ancient religions. In Binah is found Hera, queen of Olympus, Frigga of Asgard, the Egyptian Isis and any number of oriental and Celtic goddesses. It is interesting to note that an alternative symbol for Binah is a throne, the very same as the name-hieroglyph for the goddess Isis. Binah is called "The Mother of Mothers." She lies behind creation and in her is found the potential of everything that can, and could exist.

The symbols of Binah are feminine and receptive in nature; the cup, the cauldron, the circle, the oval and the diamond. Everything that is inert, stable and unchanging is said to partake of the nature of Binah. In astrology, Binah is associated with Saturn, the ponderous, slow planet of time itself.

These three Sephirot form the topmost triangle of the Tree of Life. It is the only triangle of the Tree that is upward pointing, towards the ultimate and unknowable. The three are known as the "Supernals." To the Renaissance Qabalists, this primal trinity was suggestive of the familiar "Father, Son and Holy Ghost" of Christian theology.

Below the Supernals is the abyss, yet crossing this yawning cosmic chasm, the emanations continue, as Chockmah, or wisdom, gives rise to Hesed or love. This is the first emanation of the second or ethical triangle (downward pointing). In turn, Binah, or Understanding, is made manifest in Geburah, the fifth emanation. Now the formless achieves form and the polarity of Hesed and its opposite Geburah symbolizes the interplay of creation and destruction that is only to be found in the physical universe. In many ways, the ethical triangle can be thought of as a father, a mother and a child, as the Sephirot begin their approach to the human level.

The Fourth Sphere—Hesed, Love

Hesed is the fourth of the Sephirot, expressing the concept of love. However, this is not personal affection but a gentle, unconditional love that cares for all existence. Hesed is a kindly force, the protective yet firm authority of a father guiding a child. This is also the force that systematically guides the course of evolution as well as more personal development. Here we find the concepts of law and order, of civilization, peace, justice and benevolence.

Like its "father" Chockmah, the symbols of Hesed are phallic in nature; the royal scepter, a bishop's crosier, a magician's wand and a shepherd's crook, all emblems of authority. The horn of the unicorn is also associated with Hesed as an emblem of virility. Emotive symbols such as the pyramid, possibly representing the structure of society, and the equal-armed cross are also associated with Hesed, both being particularly apt images for the fourth Sephira. Hesed is connected to the astrological planet Jupiter and Hesed may be imagined as a noble king seated upon a cubic throne.

The Fifth Sphere—Geburah, Power

On the same level, but diametrically opposed to Hesed, is Geburah, astrologically governed by the planet Mars. Its nature is destructive, symbolizing a wrathful and fierce divine force eliminating the useless, so that more progressive forms may prosper. Aleister Crowley was of the opinion that the best image of Geburah was the Hindu goddess Kali, the terrible mother, devourer of her children and drinker of blood. In this sense Geburah can be understood as the force of extinction. As Hesed builds up, so Geburah destroys.

The emotions associated with this Sephira are likewise destructive; hatred, cruelty, violence, war and revenge. In short, Geburah is a predator. As Hesed is the force of evolution, so Geburah expresses the idea of "Nature red in tooth and claw." The fearsome basilisk, a mythical beast whose very glance was deadly and whose breath was venomous, symbolizes Geburah.

All the symbolism of Geburah harks back to this intrinsic violence. Among its emblems are the sword, the flail and the chains of subjugation. Its very number, five, is associated with upheaval and rebellion, its guardian angel is given as Sammael, the very same being who is identified with Satan himself.

The interaction between the kindly Hesed and the violent Geburah is seen as a necessary conflict. This is an important point; it was not seen as a struggle between good and evil, but rather as an expression of absolute necessity in the ways of nature and the universe.

It is also interesting to note that the crook and flail emblems of Hesed and Geburah respectively were used as the symbols of monarchy in ancient Egypt, standing for the pharaoh's prerogative to guide and to punish as he saw fit. However, only when we get to Tiphareth, the next Sephira in the sequence, do we see equilibrium between these opposing forces emerge.

The Sixth Sphere—Tiphareth, Beauty

The paths from Hesed and Geburah meet at the lowest point of the ethical triangle in Tiphareth, the sphere of beauty, in the "child" position. This is also considered to be the sphere of the "Savior" and of "The god who dies and rises again." The most obvious correlation here is to Christ Himself, but it should not be forgotten that other, more ancient deities were also believed to have died and been resurrected. In ancient Egyptian theology, Ra the sun god died each evening, only to be reborn at dawn. Osiris, the husband of Isis, was also killed and raised again. In Greek mythology, Adonis and Hercules were slain and reborn, while in Norse myth, the beloved solar deity Baldur sojourned in the underworld before returning to the light.

Tiphareth is astrologically governed by the Sun, and is the reflection of Kether, which "surpasseth the Sun." It is in solar symbolism that the ferocity of Geburah and the nurturing of Hesed find their balance, because the Sun can radiate its benevolence and kindly warmth or wither and blast with its heat. Tiphareth is also said to be the highest sphere on the Tree that the human mind can attain in a normal state of consciousness. Its primary symbol is the phoenix, standing for rebirth and eternal life.

The third and bottom-most triangle of the Tree is known as the astral triangle. It begins with Netzah or Endurance, and its opposite is Hod or Majesty. At the center of the triangle lies Yesod, the sphere of Foundation, and at the base is the physical world itself, which is known as Malkuth the Kingdom.

The Seventh Sphere—Netzah, Endurance

Netzah is the sphere of animal drives, expressing the concept of attraction, of desire, passion and instinctive actions. Here is the force of nature itself, of the "fight or flight" instinct, the physical passions and the urge to procreate. Netzah expresses the invincibility of the natural world. In terms of humanity, this sphere relates to every impulse that is instinctive, emotional and sensual. Thought does not come into it; that function is found in the opposing sphere, Hod.

This Sephira is astrologically governed by Venus, the planet of desire and of love. In symbolic terms, the animals most associated with the Sephira are those of the cat family (with the exception of the lion, which is solar in nature and thus belongs to Tiphareth). The spotted lynx is usually cited as the beast of Netzah, but the leopard and the jaguar may also be included. The connection with the leopard is very interesting, because this animal was held to be the companion of the Greek god Dionysus, better known as the Roman Bacchus. As well as governing drunkenness, this deity was the god of unreason and of wild abandon. His orgiastic worship was said to release the soul of his devotees from the burdens of civilization.

The Eighth Sphere—Hod, Majesty

The Sephira in opposite position to Netzah is Hod, the Sephira of the mind. This sphere governs rationality and logic rather than instinct. It is here that we first find the contrived and the artificial, the products of the mind of man rather than the creation of God.

In astrological terms, this sphere is governed by Mercury and stands for the powers of mental creativity, imagination and insight. It should be noted that the Qabalists viewed these mental faculties, which we value so highly, with suspicion. For them a logical approach tended to obscure the truth rather than leading to it. The phrase that comes to mind is "Intellectual arrogance," a belief that because we know so much that we already know it all. It was also believed that upbringing, education and training served to repress the natural instincts, which are basically good. It should be remembered that it was a serpent that tempted Eve to eat of the tree of knowledge and thereby caused the fall of man from paradise. And indeed, a serpent or even twin serpents entwined about a herald's staff is the main symbol for this sphere.

Be that as it may, the influence of the canny Mercury here represents ingenuity and an ability to solve problems, albeit that it can also promote guile and deceitfulness.

The Ninth Sphere—Yesod, Foundation

The central Sephira of this triangle is Yesod, the Foundation. This is the sphere of change, of growth and decay, increase and decrease. It is governed by the inconstant Moon and, like its celestial counterpart, is mysterious and magical. Yesod is often thought of as being dark and possibly sinister, representing the unconscious mind, yet we should bear in mind that the Moon illuminates the darkness so that the truth may be seen.

Yesod is a combination of the instinctive drives of Netzah and the power of reason represented by Hod. Understanding of this sphere promises high spiritual achievement, and symbolizes the boundless potentials inherent within the self. Yesod is the ninth sphere and this number symbolizes initiation into the mysteries of the occult. In mythology, the Moon is considered to be the mistress of magic and witchcraft; therefore Yesod represents the hidden forces at work in our lives.

It might seem strange that the symbolic animal of Yesod is the lumbering elephant, yet this great beast combines enormous strength with great intelligence. In the vegetable kingdom, this sphere is represented by the mandrake, a plant steeped in superstition and folklore. The mandrake was considered to be one of the most powerful ingredients of magic.

The Tenth Sphere—Malkuth, the Kingdom

The lowest of the Sephira is Malkuth the Kingdom, our own world, or to be more correct, the world that we perceive with our physical senses. It is the least spiritual of the ten spheres, being the furthest away from the "First Mover," Kether.

Malkuth also represents the mind of man. It is also thought to be a feminine part of God, called the Shekinah, which has fallen from the heights of spirituality and is now imprisoned within matter itself. Therefore the implication that a portion of the Divine is exiled from itself. Thus, this world is the place of "hard knocks," where arduous lessons have to be learned. A further implication being that the great task of understanding the Qabalah is to reunite the material with the spiritual and therefore to restore the wholeness of the Divine.

In keeping with this sentiment, the symbolic beast of Malkuth is the enigmatic sphinx. The sphinx referred to is not the famous Egyptian one at Giza, but the Greek version, which was said to haunt a rock above the city of Thebes and demand that travelers answer her riddle. The Greek sphinx combined the head of a woman with the body of a lion, the wings of an eagle and the hindquarters of a bull. In this manner, she represented the four elements, the four directions and the four fixed signs of the zodiac.

The riddle she asked was, "What has four legs in the morning, two at noon and three at eventide?" The answer to this was "man." The sphinx also symbolizes the very concept of a riddle, the greatest riddle of all being: "What is the meaning of life, and what is man's place in it?" This is the very mystery that the Qabalah in particular and religion and philosophy in general, attempt to answer.

The sphere of Malkuth has no astrological association, since it symbolizes the earth itself.

The Influence of the Hermetica

The Renaissance scholars who discovered the Jewish Qabalah immediately noticed a correlation between the Sephirot and their own familiar image of the universe as a set of nine concentric crystal spheres centered on the earth. This universal view was derived from the first century A.D. writings of Claudius Ptolemaius, or Ptolemy, the so-called Ptolemaic cosmos. According to Ptolemy, the outermost of the celestial spheres was Heaven itself, within this circle, and serving to conceal it, was the starry sky. The stars themselves were considered to be pinprick holes through which the glorious light of heaven could be dimly perceived. Within this sphere of the stars lay the sphere of Saturn, within that was the sphere of Jupiter and so on through Mars, the Sun, Venus, Mercury and, closest to the earth, the Moon, making seven "planetary" spheres in all.

In the Renaissance, it was a standard belief of both churchmen and Hermetic scholars alike that every human soul came from God and descended to the earthly plane via these planetary spheres, gaining astrological characteristics from each in turn. The sphere of Saturn provided a sense of duty; wisdom came from Jupiter, aggression from Mars and so on. Those of a Hermetic turn of mind found that it was theoretically possible to turn this concept on its head and envisage a journey from the earth plane to the most spiritual levels, seeking personal enlightenment.

However, a journey that would involve climbing the rungs of this planetary "ladder" would need a route map, and in the pathways of the Tree of Life these mystics found the answer that they needed. This was because, just as the creative force had descended the Tree of Life from the "First Mover" to the material Kingdom, surely it was possible for the pure seeker after truth to retrace those steps to gain illumination. It is this concept that gives the 22 pathways joining the Sephirot of the Tree of Life their profound significance.

The Pathways of the Tree of Life

According to the Tree of Life diagram, the ten Sephirot are connected together by 22 pathways, each symbolized by a letter of the Hebrew alphabet. Thus the first pathway from Kether to Chockmah is linked to "aleph," the first letter of the Hebrew script, the second to "beth" and so on.

To each letter is ascribed a meaning, a numerical value and a "virtue," the symbolic essence of which is derived from its position in the Tree of Life scheme as shown in the Tree of Life Summary.

The Tarot and the Tree

It was an apparent coincidence that alerted a Parisian wig maker and part-time fortune-teller named Alliette to the relationship of Tarot cards to the mysteries of the Qabalah. Inspired by the work of Antoine de Court de Gebelin in 1781, Alliette reasoned that the 22 cards of the Major Arcana must be related to the 22 letters of the Hebrew alphabet, and therefore to the 22 paths of the Tree of Life itself.

Alliette is a fascinating figure. A wig maker in an age of extravagant fashion, he added to his reputation, and doubtless his popularity amongst his aristocratic clientele, by claiming that he had been a pupil of the enigmatic Count St. Germain. St. Germain had haunted the royal courts of Europe some time before (and some would say since). He was a self-proclaimed immortal who claimed to have discovered the elixir of eternal youth, could transmute metals, was a master of the mystic arts, and who may have been the Wandering Jew of legend himself.

For his part, Alliette supplemented his income by creating horoscopes, reading palms, practicing numerology, selling lucky charms and, more importantly for our purposes, interpreting Tarot cards. The writings of Court de Gebelin were a revelation to him, even though he later claimed to have anticipated de Gebelin's findings and imaginatively added to them. Alliette proclaimed that the Tarot had been designed exactly 171 years after Noah's flood, at a temple three leagues from the Egyptian city of Memphis.

Tree of Life Summary

Pathway (in descending order)	Hebrew Letter	Numerical Value	Meaning
1 (Kether to Chockmah)	Aleph (A)	1	Ox / Air
2 (Kether to Binah)	Beth (B)	2	House
3 (Kether to Tiphareth)	Gimel (G)	3	Camel
4 (Chockmah to Binah)	Daleth (D)	4	Door
5 (Chockmah to Tiphareth)	He (H)	5	Window
6 (Chockmah to Hesed)	Vau (U, V)	6	Nail
7 (Binah to Tiphareth)	Zain (Z)	7	Sword
8 (Binah to Geburah)	Cheth (Ch)	8	Fence
9 (Hesed to Geburah)	Teth (T)	9	Serpent
10 (Hesed to Tiphareth)	Yod (I, Y)	10	Hand
11 (Hesed to Netzah)	Kaph (K)	20	Palm
12 (Geburah to Tiphareth)	Lamed (L)	30	Ox-goad
13 (Geburah to Hod)	Mem (M)	40	Water
14 (Tiphareth to Netzah)	Nun (N)	50	Fish
15 (Tiphareth to Yesod)	Samekh (S)	60	Crutch / Support
16 (Tiphareth to Hod)	Ayin (O)	70	Eye
17 (Netzah to Hod)	Pe (P)	80	Mouth
18 (Netzah to Yesod)	Tzaddi (Tz)	90	Fishhook
19 (Netzah to Malkuth)	Qoph (Q)	100	Back of the head
20 (Hod to Yesod)	Resh (R)	200	Head
21 (Hod to Malkuth)	Shin (Sh)	300	Tooth / Fire
22 (Yesod to Malkuth)	Tau (Th)	400	Cross

Seventeen wise sages accomplished the task, taking a further four years to complete it. Hermes Trismagestus himself had conceived the plan, and, since this figure was thought to be the equivalent of the Egyptian god of wisdom, Thoth, this is the reason the esoteric title of the cards is "The Book of Thoth." The original cards were engraved on leaves of gold, and the cards we know are but degenerate descendants of the divinely inspired original.

Alliette's own idiosyncratic version of the Tarot certainly was a degenerate descendant of the original. Writing under the pseudonym "Etteilla" (his own name spelled backwards), he altered the design and numbering of the major cards and added interpretations such as "a voyage by sea," "a lawsuit" and even "the loss of an overcoat." If the remote possibility exists that Alliette was right, then surely the boundless wisdom of Hermes Trismagestus and the seventeen sages was a wasted effort.

It took a far more imposing and authoritative figure to fit the individual cards into the coherent framework of the pathways of the Tree of Life. This was Alphonse Louis Constant (1810–1875). Constant was the son of a shoemaker and had trained for the priesthood, later becoming involved with radical politics and occult researches. He became a committed Qabalist and wrote under the name by which he is best known, that of Eliphas Levi, a pseudonym that is nothing more than translating Alphonse Louis into Hebrew.

Levi's great work was "Le Dogme et Rituel de la Haute Magic" or "The Doctrine and Ritual of Ancient Magic," published in 1856. In this tome, Levi contemptuously dismissed the work of Alliette stating, "Instead of revealing the secrets of the Tarot, Alliette had re-veiled them!"

For his own part, Levi ingeniously linked the 22 major Tarot cards to the Hebrew letters and thus to the pathways of the Tree of Life, but he didn't stop there. The four suits of the minor cards were identified with the four Hebrew letters that spelled out the unspeakable name of God as it was revealed to Moses. Following this, it seemed obvious that the cards from ace to ten were representative of the ten Sephirot.

Levi was convinced that the very name Tarot was derived from the Latin word "rota" meaning "wheel." He was of the opinion that this wheel was an early Christian emblem for Christ and that the writer of the Book of Revelations was aware of this, since this, the last book of the New Testament, has 22 chapters. Ancient Egypt was not ignored in his theories, because in apparent contradiction to his Biblical views, Levi also attributed the Tarot's origins to the writings of Iambalichus, a Neoplatonist philosopher of the fourth century A.D. who described the 22 stages of initiation into the mysteries of Osiris.

According to Levi, a picture illustrated each of these stages, and these were the origins of the images of the Major Arcana. Unfortunately for this romantic idea, no hieroglyphs resembling Tarot imagery have ever been discovered.

However romantic and imaginative Levi's theories might be, his card allocations to the 22 pathways have ensured that a link between the Tarot and the Qabalah has been taken for granted ever since.

The awkward placement of the unnumbered card the Fool between the twentieth and twenty-first cards, Judgement and the World, was hotly contested by a later writer, Samuel Liddell MacGregor Mathers. Mathers also took exception to Levi's astrological attributions of the cards (as you will see in the chapter on Tarot and astrology), and he proposed his own variation for the Golden Dawn System. It is Mather's set of attributions that have become generally accepted.

A keen-eyed reader will notice that, apart from reassigning the Fool to the first position, Mathers also switched the placements of Justice and Strength. According to Mathers, Justice should be the eleventh card instead of the eighth, and vice versa. He did this for astrological reasons—as you will see in the chapter on Tarot and astrology.

Eliphas Levi's Qabalistic Card Attributions

Pathway (in descending order)	Hebrew Letter	Card Number	Card Title
1 (Kether to Chockmah)	Aleph (A)	1	The Magician
2 (Kether to Binah)	Beth (B)	2	The High Priestess
3 (Kether to Tiphareth)	Gimel (G)	3	The Empress
4 (Chockmah to Binah)	Daleth (D)	4	The Emperor
5 (Chockmah to Tiphareth)	He (H)	5	The Hierophant
6 (Chockmah to Hesed)	Vau (U, V)	6	The Lovers
7 (Binah to Tiphareth)	Zain (Z)	7	The Chariot
8 (Binah to Geburah)	Cheth (Ch)	8	Justice
9 (Hesed to Geburah)	Teth (T)	9	The Hermit
10 (Hesed to Tiphareth)	Yod (I, Y)	10	The Wheel of Fortune
11 (Hesed to Netzah)	Kaph (K)	11	Strength
12 (Geburah to Tiphareth)	Lamed (L)	12	The Hanged Man
13 (Geburah to Hod)	Mem (M)	13	Death
14 (Tiphareth to Netzah)	Nun (N)	14	Temperance
15 (Tiphareth to Yesod)	Samekh (S)	15	The Devil
16 (Tiphareth to Hod)	Ayin (O)	16	The Tower
17 (Netzah to Hod)	Pe (P)	17	The Star
18 (Netzah to Yesod)	Tzaddi (Tz)	18	The Moon
19 (Netzah to Malkuth)	Qoph (Q)	19	The Sun
20 (Hod to Yesod)	Resh (R)	20	Judgement
21 (Hod to Malkuth)	Shin (Sh)	None	The Fool
22 (Yesod to Malkuth)	Tau (Th)	21	The World

Samuel L. M. Mathers' Qabalistic Card Attributions

Pathway (in descending order)	Hebrew Letter	Card Number	Card Title
1 (Kether to Chockmah)	Aleph (A)	None	The Fool
2 (Kether to Binah)	Beth (B)	1	The Magician
3 (Kether to Tiphareth)	Gimel (G)	2	High Priestess
4 (Chockmah to Binah)	Daleth (D)	3	The Empress
5 (Chockmah to Tiphareth)	He (H)	4	The Emperor
6 (Chockmah to Hesed)	Vau (U, V)	5	The Hierophant
7 (Binah to Tiphareth)	Zain (Z)	6	The Lovers
8 (Binah to Geburah)	Cheth (Ch)	7	The Chariot
9 (Hesed to Geburah)	Teth (T)	8	Strength
10 (Hesed to Tiphareth)	Yod (I, Y)	9	The Hermit
11 (Hesed to Netzah)	Kaph (K)	10	The Wheel of Fortune
12 (Geburah to Tiphareth)	Lamed (L)	11	Justice
13 (Geburah to Hod)	Mem (M)	12	The Hanged Man
14 (Tiphareth to Netzah)	Nun (N)	13	Death
15 (Tiphareth to Yesod)	Samekh (S)	14	Temperance
16 (Tiphareth to Hod)	Ayin (O)	15	The Devil
17 (Netzah to Hod)	Pe (P)	16	The Tower
18 (Netzah to Yesod)	Tzaddi (Tz)	17	The Star
19 (Netzah to Malkuth)	Qoph (Q)	18	The Moon
20 (Hod to Yesod)	Resh (R)	19	The Sun
21 (Hod to Malkuth)	Shin (Sh)	20	Judgement
22 (Yesod to Malkuth)	Tau (Th)	21	The World

Crowley's Star

Aleister Crowley was initially a disciple of Mathers, but an ego as huge as Crowley's could not ultimately stomach the arrogance of his master. The two even went to the lengths of fighting a lengthy "magical duel" in which both sent demons to harass the other with indeterminate effects. Even so, Crowley was inclined to accept the Golden Dawn Qabalistic scheme until he had what can only be described as a revelation. In his monumental work "The Book of Thoth," Crowley stated, "All these words of my book are aright, but Tzaddi is not the Star!" In other words, he fundamentally disagreed with one letter attribution as put forward by Mathers (not that he would have mentioned Mathers by name). So in Crowley's system the letter Tzaddi is associated with the Emperor, while the Star is allocated to He, as indeed it is in the still popular "Thoth" Tarot deck, which was designed by Aleister Crowley and executed by Lady Frieda Harris.

Climbing the Tree

From prehistoric times, tree symbolism has been a potent force in occult matters. In tribal societies, the shaman (a combination of healer, sorcerer, spirit medium and shape-shifter) will symbolize his passage through the various planes of existence by climbing the central pole of his tent. This tent pole represents the Tree of Life itself. In Norse mythology, the entire universe is imagined as being held together by the roots and branches of Yggdrasil, the great world-ash tree. Interestingly, this northern European belief system also holds that there are nine worlds hanging like fruit from the universal tree.

In a similar fashion to the ancient shamans, devotees of the Qabalah believe that it is possible to take a spiritual journey along the pathways of the Tree of Life. For many of them, the symbols to the Major Arcana provide the key and also important signposts, so that the astral traveler does not get lost while voyaging through the planes of existence.

Of course, the seeker after this profound experience begins his journey on the physical level, the sphere of Malkuth. He realizes that to explore the mysteries of the Tree, he must remove himself from the mundane affairs and sensations of this plane of existence, so a prolonged period of meditation is necessary. In the past, the yoga-like techniques of Abraham Abulafia were employed to master the body and the mind to ready them for the journey ahead. Both Samuel Liddell MacGregor Mathers and Aleister Crowley invented their own techniques for accomplishing the same purpose. Suitably prepared, the Qabalist can begin his journey by meditating on the card called The World or the Universe.

The symbolism of the pathways is explained in the individual sections dealing with the cards of the Major Arcana.

4

The Major Arcana and the Zodiac

The nineteenth-century French mystic Eliphas Levi had already connected the Major Arcana cards of the Tarot to the letters of the Hebrew alphabet, and therefore to the pathways of the Qabalistic Tree of Life. His occult thinking now took a different turn as he reasoned that, if the tarot were truly a universal system of divination, then it should also have a correlation to the ancient art of western astrology. The 22 major cards should fit the system of 12 zodiac signs plus the seven heavenly bodies known to the classical world.

To accomplish this feat of matching up the associations between the cards and classical astrology, Levi leaned rather heavily on his earlier Qabalistic discoveries. Some would say so much so, that where there is a conflict between them, then according to Levi, the Qabalah always won. As with the Qabalah, Levi saw no reason why the attributions should not begin with Card 1—The Magician or Juggler—which he had already connected with the Hebrew letter Aleph and the element of Air. Levi's full card attributions are shown here:

Eliphas Levi			
Card Number	Title	Hebrew Letter	Zodiac Correspondence
1	The Magician	Aleph	Air
2	The Priestess	Beth	Moon
3	The Empress	Gimel	Mars
4	The Emperor	Daleth	Sun
5	The Hierophant	He	Aries
6	The Lovers	Vau	Taurus
7	The Chariot	Zain	Gemini
8	Justice	Heth	Cancer
9	The Hermit	Tet	Leo
10	The Wheel of Fortune	Yod	Virgo
11	Strength	Kaph	Venus
12	The Hanged Man	Lamed	Libra
13	Death	Mem	Water
14	Temperance	Nun	Scorpio
15	The Devil	Samekh	Sagittarius
16	The Tower	Ayin	Capricorn
17	The Star	Pe	Mercury
18	The Moon	Tzaddi	Aquarius
19	The Sun	Qoph	Pisces
20	Judgement	Resh	Saturn
21	The Fool	Shin	Fire
22	The World	Tau	Jupiter

It was a good try, but I'm afraid it just doesn't work at all, when you consider that the gentle Empress equates with the violent Mars, the meek Hermit with exhibitionist Leo and the sacrificial Hanged Man with balanced Libra! All this before we consider the awkward positioning of the Fool and the card's inexplicable connection with the Fire element.

As usual, Samuel Liddell MacGregor Mathers fundamentally disagreed with Levi's views. He accepted that, just as the cards related to the Qabalah, they must logically also connect with astrology, but considered that Levi had started in the wrong place.

Mathers' attributions are given below:

Card Number	Title	Golden Dawn Attributions	Modern Variations
	Samuel Liddell MacGregor Mathers		
0	The Fool	Air	Uranus
1	The Magician	Mercury	
2	The Priestess	The Moon	
3	The Empress	Venus	
4	The Emperor	Aries	
5	The Hierophant	Taurus	
6	The Lovers	Gemini	
7	The Chariot	Cancer	
8	Strength	Leo	
9	The Hermit	Virgo	
10	The Wheel of Fortune	Jupiter	
11	Justice	Libra	
12	The Hanged Man	Water	Neptune
13	Death	Scorpio	
14	Temperance	Sagittarius	
15	The Devil	Capricorn	
16	The Tower	Mars	
17	The Star	Aquarius	
18	The Moon	Pisces	
19	The Sun	Sun	
20	Judgement	Fire	Pluto
21	The World	Saturn	

Mathers went to great lengths to tie the planets and signs of the zodiac into the Tarot system. In most cases, this series of attributions has its successes, but also has some shortcomings. For instance, only three of the four classical elements have been included since there was no space for "Earth." Originally, the three planets discovered in modern times were also left out, but are now allocated to those cards that according to Mathers were purely "elemental." Another failing of Mathers' system is that, if the zodiac is to appear in the Major Arcana in order, then Justice (originally card 8, corresponding to Libra) should not appear before Strength (originally card 11, corresponding to Leo). Mathers took the practical view and swapped them. Consequently these cards may appear in different Tarot decks in either position.

More recently, author Joseph Maxwell also proposed a system to correct the ambiguities of Mathers' system (page 46). However Maxwell's attributions don't include either the Fool or The Tower.

Some of these attributions make sense, but others definitely do not. Attributing the sign of Cancer to the Moon card is sensible, since in astrology the moon rules that sign, but why is the Hanged Man Aries? And what happened to the Dragon's Tail, the moon's southern node? It may be to answer these questions that Tarot author Brian Innes proposed a system of his own, while rejecting any Qabalistic influence on the cards at all (page 47).

Alas, the Hanged Man is still Aries, though many of the attributions do make sense. The identification of the Fool as the Part of Fortune, a theoretical point in the horoscope denoting luck, is particularly interesting.

Joseph Maxwell

Card Number	Title	Zodiac Correspondence
	The Fool	(no attribution given)
1	The Magician	Sun
2	The Priestess	Moon
3	The Empress	Venus
4	The Emperor	Jupiter
5	The Hierophant	Mercury
6	The Lovers	Sagittarius
7	The Chariot	Mars
8	Justice	Libra
9	The Hermit	Pisces
10	The Wheel of Fortune	Capricorn
11	Strength	Leo
12	The Hanged Man	Aries
13	Death	Saturn
14	Temperance	Aquarius
15	The Devil	Dragon's Head (The Moon's Northern Node)
16	The Tower	(no attribution given)
17	The Star	Taurus
18	The Moon	Cancer
19	The Sun	Gemini
20	Judgement	Scorpio
21	The World	Virgo

Brian Innes

Card Number	Title	Zodiac Correspondence
0	The Fool	The Part of Fortune
1	The Magician	Mercury
2	The Priestess	Moon
3	The Empress	Venus
4	The Emperor	Dragon's Head
5	The Hierophant	Jupiter
6	The Lovers	Sagittarius
7	The Chariot	Mars
8	Justice	Libra
9	The Hermit	Saturn
10	The Wheel of Fortune	Sun
11	Strength	Leo
12	The Hanged Man	Aries
13	Death	Dragon's Tail
14	Temperance	Aquarius
15	The Devil	Capricorn
16	The Tower	Scorpio
17	The Star	Virgo
18	The Moon	Cancer
19	The Sun	Gemini
20	Judgement	Pisces
21	The World	Taurus

MacGregor Mathers and the Golden Dawn

Pathway (in descending order)	Hebrew Letter	Card Number	Card Title	Astrological Attribution
1. (Kether to Chockmah)	Aleph (A)	None	The Fool	Air (Uranus)
2 (Kether to Binah)	Beth (B)	1	The Magician	Mercury
3 (Kether to Tiphareth)	Gimel (G)	2	The High Priestess	The Moon
4 (Chockmah to Binah)	Daleth (D)	3	The Empress	Venus
5 (Chockmah to Tiphareth)	He (H)	4	The Emperor	Aries
6 (Chockmah to Hesed)	Vau (U,V)	5	The Hierophant	Taurus
7 (Binah to Tiphareth)	Zain (Z)	6	The Lovers	Gemini
8 (Binah to Geburah)	Cheth (Ch)	7	The Chariot	Cancer
9 (Hesed to Geburah)	Teth (T)	8	Strength	Leo
10 (Hesed to Tiphareth)	Yod (I,Y)	9	The Hermit	Virgo
11 (Hesed to Netzah)	Kaph (K)	10	The Wheel of Fortune	Jupiter
12 (Geburah to Tiphareth)	Lamed (L)	11	Justice	Libra
13 (Geburah to Hod)	Mem (M)	12	The Hanged Man	Water (Neptune)
14 (Tiphareth to Netzah)	Nun (N)	13	Death	Scorpio
15 (Tiphareth to Yesod)	Samekh (S)	14	Temperance	Sagittarius
16 (Tiphareth to Hod)	Ayin (O)	15	The Devil	Capricorn
17 (Netzah to Hod)	Pe (P)	16	The Tower	Mars
18 (Netzah to Yesod)	Tzaddi (Tz)	17	The Star	Aquarius
19 (Netzah to Malkuth)	Qoph (Q)	18	The Moon	Pisces
20 (Hod to Yesod)	Resh (R)	19	The Sun	The Sun
21 (Hod to Malkuth)	Shin (Sh)	20	Judgement	Fire (Pluto)
22 (Yesod to Malkuth)	Tau (Th)	21	The World	Saturn

Even though the card attributions of Levi, Maxwell and Innes have much to commend them, it is the system of MacGregor Mathers and the Golden Dawn that has remained the accepted method of tying in the Major Arcana to the signs and planets of the zodiac. As, indeed, it has in correlating the cards to the Hebrew letters and pathways of the Qabalistic Tree of Life, and it is the system that we have used in this book. The full Golden Dawn system for the Major Arcana card correspondences is given in the following table.

The "extra" attributions given in brackets for the Fool, the Hanged Man and Judgement are very modern; dating, at the very earliest, to the 1980s. In Mathers' time, only Uranus and Neptune had been discovered. Pluto was detected in 1930. None of these remote outer worlds are counted among the classical planets of traditional astrology. For Mathers, the Golden Dawn as a whole and for Aleister Crowley, the attributions of these cards were purely related to the elements tying in with the Hebrew letters of the Qabalah.

Aleister Crowley only disputed one point in this system of attributions. In his view, although the Star should retain its correspondence to the sign of Aquarius, it should not be associated with the Hebrew letter Tzaddi, as you will see in connection with Crowley's Star.

Editor's note: Jonathan tells us that Mathers and Crowley disagreed about the cards that best suited the Hebrew letters He and Tzaddi. Mathers assigned Tzaddi to the Star, while Crowley assigned it to the Emperor and suggested that He should be used for the Star. I have the benefit of being Jewish, so I can add that the word "tzaddi" means wise or learned in the sense of having knowledge of Judaism and religious law. A righteous person, a wise person or a sage is known as a "tzaddik." Jonathan and I agree that the word would fit the Hierophant better than either the Star or the Emperor, but that this would have thrown both Mathers' and Crowley's systems out of sync.

5

The Four Grail Hallows

The commonly used modern deck of playing cards consists of four suits comprising hearts, clubs, spades and diamonds. Likewise, the Minor Arcana of the Tarot, the ancestor of the modern cards, uses Cups, Rods, Swords and Coins, with very small variations in the suit names from deck to deck.

Arthur Edward Waite, the designer of the famous Rider-Waite Tarot, the first to possess a fully illustrated set of minor cards, noticed a common theme throughout the suit symbols. He was of the opinion that there were numerous parallels between the Tarot suits and the four "Hallows" or sacred and magical objects in the legends of the Quest for the Holy Grail. This viewpoint was picked up and added to by Jessie Laidlay Weston (1850–1928) in her book "From Ritual to Romance," published in 1920. Weston was a devoted follower of the teachings of Madam Blavatsky and the Theosophist movement, as well as being a prominent member of a mystical organization called the Quest Society, which was founded in 1909.

Although the Quest Society is not considered as influential a force on modern occult thinking as the more famous Order of the Golden Dawn, many of its beliefs have infiltrated the New Age movement. In common with other more established belief systems based in the mysticism of ancient Egypt (as in the Golden Dawn), or India and the orient (as in the Theosophical Society), Weston and her compatriots in the Quest Society based many of their doctrines on the mystical traditions of western Europe; in particular, in the stirring tales of King Arthur, his Knights of the Round Table and the Quest for the Holy Grail. These themes were tied into the suit symbols of the minor cards.

The suit symbols of the Minor Arcana—the Cup, the Sword, the Rod and the Coin—are firmly established as being medieval in origin. These four most probably and most obviously represent the four classes of society in the Middle Ages in Europe. These being the priesthood symbolized by Cups, the warrior aristocracy represented by Swords, the merchant class depicted by the Coins and finally, the laboring classes or peasants by the humble Rods or Staves.

However, the reputed link between the cards and the mysterious order of the Knights Templar, as well as with the equally enigmatic heretical Gnostic sect known as the Cathars, has led to a more mystical interpretation of the suit symbols. Both these movements were active during the twelfth century in southwestern France, one of the areas put forward as the place of origin of the cards themselves.

This region, which may for convenience be called the Languedoc, is also the homeland of the troubadour tradition. The influence of these wandering minstrels and poets on the Tarot pack is evident by the inclusion of the symbolic figure of "The Magician" or "Juggler," as he was originally known. In French this card is called "Le Jongleur" or "Minstrel." One of the most popular parts of the repertoire of these itinerant bards was the stirring story of the Quest for the Holy Grail.

The earliest and possibly the best summation of this epic tale was written by a troubadour named Chretien de Troyes, who lived at the court of the Count of Champagne around 1180. The count's wife, Marie, was the daughter of the Queen of England, Eleanor of Aquitaine, a noted patroness of the arts. It is assumed that this association with the English crown inspired Chretien to translate the Arthurian romances into French, and thereby popularize them in aristocratic circles. His greatest work is Le Conte du Graal, an unfinished compilation of early Welsh and Breton legends featuring the adventures of such names as Sir Gawain and, the true hero of the story, Sir Perceval of Wales.

Sir Perceval of Wales

According to Chretien's epic tale, a mother who had lost her husband and other sons in various battles brought up Perceval in obscurity in the mountains of North Wales. For this reason the boy was kept in ignorance of the violent world beyond the soaring crags of their home. She had never told him of chivalry or of knights and their battles, or of the church and its doctrines, although she had given him a little information about God and the angels. More remarkably than this, his mother had never even told him what his name was or given any detail about his ancestry. The naïve boy only knew himself as "fair son."

One day while "fair son" was out in the forest he saw five knights of King Arthur's court, splendid in their shining armor. He immediately mistook them for angels and, bursting with curiosity questioned them. They explained who and what they were, and immediately the boy conceived the idea of finding King Arthur, becoming a knight and performing noble deeds. He ran home to his mother and told her of his discovery. Tearfully she tried to dissuade him from leaving, but the boy soon set off in rustic clothes, riding an ancient sag-bellied nag. In his haste, the boy did not think to pause when he looked back to see his mother sink to the ground as if dead.

There follows a series of slightly comic episodes that serve to illustrate "fair son's" ignorance of the world. Eventually the boy found King Arthur at his court at Carlisle. However the king did not think that "fair son" was ready for knighthood, so the boy set off once more to prove himself. Before long, the boy had carved out a reputation as a formidable fighter, but it was the general opinion that he was uncouth and probably simple-minded. However the boy's sincerity and valor did impress a certain Sir Gornemant, who tutored him in the ways of the world, gave him the name of Perceval and bestowed on him the honor of knighthood. A piece of advice Gornemant gave to Perceval was not to chatter so much and to curb his tendency to ask silly questions. It is at this stage that Perceval decided to visit his mother; however, a series of adventures follow which delay his visit; the most notable of these is Perceval's encounter with the Fisher King.

One day Perceval came to a river and there saw a small boat with two men in it. The elder was fishing, but he paused from this activity to tell Perceval that there was no way of crossing the water, so he offered him the hospitality of his castle for the night.

The fisherman turned out to be a king who had been wounded in the thigh (later writers drawing on the same source material as Chretien give the Fisher King the name Brons. This name is significant, as we shall see). The king's wound had never healed, and in consequence, movement had become difficult. So the king diverted himself by fishing while his country went to wrack and ruin. So much so that it became known as the Waste-Land.

In the feasting hall, the Fisher King presented Perceval with a wonderful sword, saying that it was the sword's destiny that it should belong to him. A young man then entered the room bearing a lance. From its tip a single drop of blood ran down the shaft onto the young man's hand. Perceval was curious but remembering Gornemant's advice did not ask any questions. There followed a strange procession of two Pages carrying a golden candelabrum, a beautiful, richly dressed girl bearing a golden chalice studded with gems, and another maiden holding a silver carving dish. Perceval's eyes were drawn to the chalice which, as it entered the hall, illuminated it with such radiance that the candles were dimmed. Silently the group crossed the room to disappear through a doorway on the other side. Perceval was amazed and could scarcely conceal his curiosity but still managed to hold his tongue.

Later a sumptuous meal was served, and during each course, the magical implements again were passed before Perceval. With superhuman effort Perceval remained silent but resolved to ask one of the young men the meaning of this marvel the next day. However when he awoke the next morning he found the castle to be deserted so he mounted his horse and rode away pondering the meaning of all he had seen.

In a later adventure, a rescued damsel explained that Perceval was meant to ask why the lance bled and was appalled to discover that the "Fair son" had neither asked that question nor the purpose of the Grail. The lady dubbed him Perceval the Unfortunate and told him that if he had asked the right questions, then the Fisher King would have been healed and the land would have again become fertile. From this point onward, in every adventure, Perceval is criticized again and again for failing to seize his opportunities at the Fisher King's castle. Eventually Perceval consults a wise hermit, who tells him that his troubles stem from the death of his mother, who had pined away, longing for the return of her son. According to the hermit, this was the sin that had tied his tongue and stopped him from fulfilling his destiny. The hermit went on to say that there were two kings in the castle, the Fisher King himself and his father, and that it was the old king who was served by the Grail. This king was such a spiritual being that a single mass wafer sufficed to give him all the nourishment that he needed. Inspired by this, Perceval was determined to seek the Grail and heal the Fisher King and his land.

It is assumed that Chretien de Troyes died before he could complete the tale, so we will never know whether Perceval put everything to rights in this version. Other writers, such as Diderot and Wolfram von Eschenbach embellished the themes of the Conte du Graal and were in no doubt of the hero's eventual success. They also were keen to add to the story by naming the Fisher King, changing the sequence and number of the marvelous objects known as the Grail Hallows, and sometimes even changing the identity of the central character to Galahad or Lancelot. Nevertheless, there can be little doubt that it was Perceval who was meant to find the Grail.

This is, however, the central theme of the Grail Hallows that has been preserved in the Tarot deck. It will be remembered that

Perceval was first presented with a superb sword. Then there followed a youth bearing a bleeding lance, followed by two more carrying a candelabrum. The radiant Grail itself then follows, borne by a richly dressed maiden, and then a silver dish carried by another beautiful girl. So here we have a sword, a lance, a cup and a round dish reminiscent of a coin. All the Tarot seems to lack is a candelabrum. It is interesting to note that American science-fiction author Piers Anthony echoes this view, and has proposed that there is an entire suit missing from the deck. The proponents of this idea have entitled these "missing" cards the suit of "Lamps" or "Aura," addressed in what they termed "The Animation Tarot."

The Fisher King

Even though many troubadours and monks were keen to give the Fisher King a noble and impeccably Christian heritage, even going so far as to make him a nephew or grandson of Joseph of Arimathea, who brought the Holy Grail to Britain. By the Middle Ages, this Biblical character was considered to be the uncle of Jesus, so the Fisher King would be Christ's cousin. However, there is reason to believe that the whole of the Grail mythos has a pagan rather than a Christian origin.

Although Chretien de Troyes does not name the Fisher King, later writers identify the maimed monarch as Brons. This name is a medieval corruption of Bran (a word meaning "raven"), a gigantic figure who is one of the main characters in Welsh mythology. In the second Branch of the epic Mabinogion, Bran is not only described as a giant, but also as the king of all Britain. Bran is also called the "Blessed" and is the owner of a magical cauldron that has the ability of restoring the dead to life, even though, after their resurrection they lose the faculty of speech.

In the course of the Mabinogion story, Bran is wounded in the thigh by a spear, a wound that cannot be healed. By his own request, he is later beheaded, his head remaining miraculously alive. His last wish is to be buried under the White Hill in London, facing towards the continent, to provide a charm against foreign invasion. The site of the White Hill is actually occupied by the Tower of London, where Bran's six sacred ravens still keep their vigil. In keeping with the traditional tale, it is said that should these ravens depart the Tower, then Britain will fall soon after. To prevent such an eventuality, these fat, spoiled scavenging birds have their wings clipped to make their escape unlikely.

The Grail Castle

Another Grail connection to the mythical divine king Bran dates from the Middle Ages. The fortress of Dinas Bran (translated as "The Citadel of Bran" or "The Citadel of the Raven"), perched high on a crag above the town of Llangollen, was commonly thought to be the Grail Castle of Chretien's tale.

The fact that this imposing ruin is close to Snowdonia, Perceval's supposed place of origin, adds an evocative quality to the legend. If Dinas Bran were to be identified with the Grail Castle, then it would mean that Perceval encountered the Fisher King on the banks of the River Dee that flows in the valley below. This river was once renowned for the quality of its salmon, a fish that symbolized wisdom in Celtic beliefs.

The Grail of God

The Holy Grail, most often thought to be a cup or drinking vessel, was clearly identified as the cup from which Christ drank at the Last Supper. It was also used to collect His blood as He hung upon the cross. This vessel was also thought to be the property of Joseph of Arimathea, a rich merchant who may, or may not, have been an uncle of the Virgin Mary and of Jesus.

Medieval legend has it that Joseph of Arimathea traded in tin with Cornwall, in the far Southwest of the British mainland, and it is to that locality he fled when the Romans persecuted the earliest Christians. From his landing point, he and a few followers made their way to Glastonbury in Somerset, where they founded the first Christian Church in Europe. It was this small chapel that eventually became the foundation for Glastonbury Abbey, which in turn was reputed to be the very Isle of Avalon, the burial place of King Arthur himself.

Another version of the story became popular in France. In this variation, Joseph of Arimathea merely provides transportation for the Grail and its keeper, Mary Magdalene, to the south of France. It is this version of the tale that has given rise to a whole new phenomenon, the mystery of Rennes le Chateau, and the possibility that if the Grail is to be understood as a container for blood, then it is actually symbolic of a particular bloodline. This bloodline is claimed to be that of the ancient Merovingian kings of France, who (so the theory goes), were direct descendants of Jesus and Mary Magdalene. The Order of the Knights Templar in turn is claimed to have been the protector of this sacred heritage and therefore guardian of the Grail itself.

One "proof" put forward for this theory is the manner in which the words "Holy Grail" were often rendered in medieval French as "San Greal" or "Holy Vessel." However, if one letter is shifted, it becomes "Sang Real" or "Royal Blood."

Be that as it may, in public imagination, the Holy Grail became the ultimate of sacred relics in an age when the bones of even the most minor saint were objects of veneration. How much more important was an artifact that was used by Christ at the Last Supper, and which had held his blood, and which indeed had been the cup of the very first communion?

The stories of the wondrous Grail became elaborated with time. If its sacred credentials were not already impressive enough, the cup soon became thought of as being made of a single emerald, which had once been the central gem in the crown of Lucifer when he was the chief of the angels. At Lucifer's fall, the gem, symbolizing pride, fell to earth and had been possessed by many arrogant Biblical villains such as Nimrod, the Pharaoh of the Exodus and wicked King Herod, before achieving its redemption at the table of the highest king of all, Christ.

If, however, the distorting lens of medieval Christianity is removed and spurious connections with Biblical characters are put aside, we are left with a wonder-working vessel, probably in the form of a cup or chalice. But what miracles were credited to the power of the Grail?

Firstly, many sources, including that of Chretien de Troyes, refer to the Grail as a provider of food. It usually appears at a feast and we are told that a single mass wafer from the cup nourishes the Fisher King's father. The Grail is also connected with healing, because if Perceval had had the wit to ask the right questions, the Fisher King and all his land would have been made whole again and undergone a form of rebirth. Finally, the Grail has something to do with spiritual enlightenment, because in all the quest stories, the hero, be he Perceval, Galahad or some other intrepid knight, achieves divine inspiration at the culmination of the tale.

These beliefs are derived in part from the cauldron or rebirth, which was owned by Bran, but they also have much in common with other vessels found in the native mythologies of Britain and Ireland. The earliest record we have of one of these is the Cauldron of the Dagda. Dagda was a father-god in Irish mythology, and, like Bran, was considered to be a giant. Dagda's cauldron provided all that was best to eat and drink in his hall. This cauldron was one of the treasures of the People of Dana, the Celtic gods who brought these treasures to earth from their mysterious homelands. It was said that the cauldron itself had been made in the West, in the distant mythical city of Finias.

Across the Irish Sea in Wales, the witch Ceridwen (herself a dim reflection of a Celtic goddess) brewed a "Cauldron of Inspiration" for a year and a day so that her stupid, ugly son Afagddu would achieve enlightenment. In another story written in the Dark Ages, King Arthur himself entered the Otherworld to win a magical cauldron, thereby becoming among the first who sought a Grail.

In an equally symbolic vein, the alchemists of the Middle Ages and the Renaissance periods were quick to note the similarity between the Grail stories and their own quest for the philosopher's stone and the elixir of life.

So our image of the Holy Grail is an amalgam of the very cup used by Our Lord and the potent vessels or rebirth, plenty and inspiration employed by Celtic gods and heroes. In fact, the major difference between this, the supreme Christian and pagan relic and all other holy memorabilia, was that the Grail could not be found. The same could not be said of another of the Grail Hallows—the spear, because that artifact has a well-known and quite bloody history.

The Spear of Destiny

According to Christian tradition, a blind Roman centurion commonly named Longinus, but otherwise known as Gaius Cassius, thrust his lance into Jesus' side as He hung upon the cross. The blood that poured forth entered the eyes of Longinus and cured his blindness. Since that day, the spear of Longinus was regarded as a relic of awesome power. However, its main miraculous virtue was not the ability to heal, but the ability to rule. Legend has it that whoever possesses it will become a great conqueror, if not ruler of the world. For this reason, the martial relic became known as the Spear of Destiny.

As usual in these matters, monkish chroniclers backdated the history of the spear beyond its ownership by the centurion Longinus. Some claimed that it had been made by the prophet Phineas and was successively owned by Joshua, King Saul and Herod the Great (he also apparently owned the Grail itself at one time too).

In the time since the crucifixion, the lance passed from hand to hand, being owned by the Emperors Constantine the Great, Justinian and Charlemagne. Many rulers of the Holy Roman Empire used the spear as a talisman of victory, and from them, the relic passed into the possession of the Habsburg dynasty of Austria.

The power that possession of the spear imparts is only one half of the story. It is true that it was believed that he who wielded it would hold the balance of power in the world, but to lose it was fatal. According to legend the great warrior kings, Charlemagne and Frederick Barbarossa, both died soon after dropping the spear, as indeed did many other owners of the weapon. Only the centurion Longinus himself is said to have escaped this fate—only to be visited by a worse one. Because of his crime of slaying Christ, Longinus was condemned to walk the earth as an immortal until the day of doom. His legend goes on to say that he can only escape this dreadful curse by being struck down by the hand of one who bears the spear itself.

In more modern times, belief in the legend of the spear has proved to be a lure to megalomaniac dictators. The Austrians successfully concealed the relic from Napoleon Bonaparte in 1806 and refused the German Kaiser's demand for it in 1913. However another would-be world conqueror, Adolf Hitler, was more successful than his predecessors.

Adolf Hitler was a believer in the power of the spear and in his own destiny. He first saw it in 1909, and if he is to be believed, received a vision that he could conquer the world with the Spear of Destiny in his possession. By 1938 it was his, but the advance of American troops on Nuremburg on April 30, 1945 finally ended the fortunes of Hitler and the Nazi party. The ancient lance was discovered in a vault under the town at just about the same time that Hitler took his own life in the Berlin bunker. On the direct orders of General Eisenhower, the relic was returned to Vienna, but in the period while the spear was in the possession of American authorities, the United States dropped atomic bombs on Hiroshima and Nagasaki, changing the balance of power in the world forever.

Only the point of the lance now remains, in pride of place in the Habsburg treasury in the Hofburg museum, Vienna. The wooden spear-shaft is long gone. In appearance, the remnant of the weapon is nothing more than a damaged Roman blade held together by threads of gold, silver and bronze, which also serve to bind this awesome relic to an alleged nail from the True Cross. The addition of this nail may have been to retain the holiness of the spearhead after the all-important shaft had rotted away. After all, it is the shaft of the lance rather than the head that is found in the Minor Arcana of the Tarot, masquerading as the Ace of Wands.

Putting both pious and historical legends aside, the Spear of Destiny, like the more famous Grail, is likely to derive from Celtic mythology rather than from any of the events surrounding the crucifixion. Spears of wondrous magical power were a feature of the stories of the ancient Celts of Britain and Ireland. The identification of the Fisher King, Brons, with the mythological giant, Bran, provides one clue, because a spear had caused the wound that would not heal. Much of the action of Bran's story takes place in Ireland, and it is to Irish mythology that we must turn for an example of a magical spear.

The gods of early Ireland were known as the People of Dana or Tuatha de Dannan, a shining race of heroes with superhuman powers. One of the foremost of these was Lugh, the sun god, whose primary attribute was his spear, which represented a ray of light. The spear was the second of the magical implements that the People of Dana brought with them from their homelands. In this case, the spear was said to have been made in the South, in the mythical city of Gorias.

Another spear endowed with mystical properties is found in the fourth branch of the Welsh Mabinogion as a means of killing Llew, the Welsh version of Lugh. This weapon had to be made under very special circumstances. The influence of Christianity is evident here, because the death-dealing blade must be "forged on a Sunday while a priest is saying Mass." Symbolically, it is a weapon of this type that wounded Bran, and it is therefore the descendant of this spear that was borne before Perceval in the Fisher King's castle, a single drop of blood still upon its blade.

The Sword of Power

In the lore of medieval Europe, the sword was the most potent symbol of nobility, courage and authority. At the time that Chretien de Troyes wrote his Grail story, the sword had become the symbol both of justice and of righteousness, so much so that to the barons and knights who fought in the Holy Land, it was almost as important an image as the cross of Christ. The crusader crosses worn on the vestments of the knightly orders such as the Templars can be easily mistaken for inverted swords, symbolic of both righteousness and force.

It is not surprising therefore, that magical swords became standard ingredients in many hero tales of the crusading period. In Chretien's version of the Perceval legend, the Fisher King gives the hero a sword immediately upon his arrival at the Grail Castle. As usual, this detail was embellished by other writers who were quick to state that this weapon had once belonged to the Biblical King David, and had been the very blade that he had taken from the fallen giant Goliath, and with which he had struck off the villain's head. This is an interesting point, both in connection with the archetypal Celtic theme of a severed head and in terms of the Tarot suit of Swords. Some old French packs of cards allocated the name of "David" to the King of Swords or Spades.

Other Grail questers were also reputed to possess wondrous swords. In the story of Sir Galahad, a Merlinesque hermit shows the brave knight a sword embedded in a stone that miraculously floats on water. Sir Galahad, like Arthur before him, drew the sword from the stone, thereby proving that the weapon was destined for him alone.

King Arthur, of course, was reputed to possess the most wonderful magical sword of all, the glorious Excalibur. So famous was this weapon that no less than two versions of its origin exist. The first is the well-known story of the boy Arthur proving his rightness for the throne of Britain by freeing it from the stone in which Merlin had placed it. The other tale, equally well known, is of how Merlin took Arthur to a lake where he saw an arm "clothed in white samite" rising from the water holding a sword of incomparable beauty. The story goes on to tell of how the sword had been forged by the Lady of the Lake (another example of a thinly veiled Celtic lake goddess), and that when Arthur's days were done, it was to be returned to her. Indeed, after the Battle of Camlann,

Arthur's last and fatal victory, his close companion Sir Bedevere cast the sword into the water, only to see the white arm again rise, brandish the sword three times and then sink with it into the depths.

In both versions of the tale, the mysterious figure of Merlin the magician is prominent. This is an interesting feature because this most mighty of enchanters was reputed to guard a series of objects known as "The Thirteen Treasures of Britain," which may be forerunners of the Grail Hallows. One of these is a blade called "Dyrnwyn" or "White Hilt." It had belonged to a hero known as Rhydderch the Generous, and its magical properties were that if a brave man drew it the sword would burst into flame. If wielded by a coward, however, the blade would remain dull and lifeless. The sword was also reputed to be able to fly to the hand of its owner when he called for it. Legend has it that all thirteen treasures are kept in a glass house on the island of Bardsey off the coast of North Wales, where they will remain forever.

It is evident that "Dyrnwyn" in the keeping of Merlin is the mythological ancestor of our familiar Excalibur. The name Excalibur literally means "Out of Calibur" or even "Made in Calibur." Calibur has therefore been taken to be the realm of the Lady of the Lake. However, this is not the first or even the most traditional name by which the sword was known. To the Welsh originators of the legends, the sword of power was "Caledfwlch." It is certainly with a weapon of this name that according to the sixth-century poem, "The Spoils of Annwn," that Arthur braved the perils of the Otherworld, "Annwn," to claim the Cauldron of Plenty. The hero accomplished this feat in the company of his faithful war-band; one of whom was a character called Bedwyr the one-handed, the original of the medieval Sir Bedevere.

According to Irish lore, the Sword of Power was one of the magical implements of the Tuatha de Dannaan or People of Dana. Their traditions state that this weapon was forged in the city (or island) of Murias in the East.

The Stone of Kings

When we come to the "Coin" equivalent in the story of Perceval, we note that the silver dish borne through the hall of the Fisher King is the fourth of the Grail Hallows. In Chretien's version of the tale, this object represents an empty platter. However, later writers state that the dish contained a human head. This head was usually identified as belonging to either St. John the Baptist (beheaded by Herod Antipas in payment for the dance of Salome), or that of St. Paul, whose martyrdom was at the command of Nero.

As we have previously seen, these Biblical associations often mask an older, pagan Celtic symbolism. In this case, the disputed head is probably that of Bran himself. Bran, according to the second branch of the Welsh epic "The Mabinogion," after being wounded by the spear, was decapitated by his own choice. His head remaining miraculously alive for eighty years on an Otherworld island before being buried on the White Hill in London as a talisman against foreign invasion.

However, if we take our cue from the other magical objects found in Irish tradition, a stone takes the place of the dish. It is said that this stone had been shaped in the North, in the city of Falias. This is a particularly interesting departure, because the Tarot suit of Coins is usually taken to represent the element Earth, and in several modern Tarot decks, the suit is replaced by that of "Stones." Nevertheless, while we are still concerned with Irish mythology, there is a point of confusion, because some early sources say that it was a circular shield rather than a stone that was made in Falias. The reason for this confusion may be found in the practice of "king-making," as we shall see.

Like the Spear of Destiny, this treasure still exists. Its earliest history in ancient Ireland is well documented. It was called the "Lia Fail" or Stone of Destiny. Its mythological place of origin was the city of Falias and hence the object was sometimes known as the Stone of Fal. By ancient custom, the High-Kings of Ireland stood upon the stone during their coronation at the Hill of Tara, and indeed the stone was supposed to cry out in approval when the rightful monarch took his place upon it. The "Lia Fail" was transported to Scotland in the sixth century for the inauguration of Fergus the Great, brother to the Irish High-King. Fergus had begged his elder sibling for the use of it. After the event, the wily Fergus neglected to return the relic to Ireland, and instead transported it to Scone Abbey where it rested for over six hundred years, becoming known as The Stone of Scone. In 1297, the English King Edward I captured the stone and brought it as a trophy of war to London, where it became the Coronation Stone in Westminster Abbey. From that point onward, every English monarch has been crowned while seated on a chair that incorporates the stone. There is no record, however, that the "Lia Fail" has ever cried out its approval in historical times.

An ancient prophecy states that wherever the stone is, a king of Scottish blood will follow. This was certainly the case in 1603 when King James VI of Scotland ascended the English throne to unite the two kingdoms. James could trace his ancestry back to King Fergus the Great, and it is a fact that every succeeding monarch has been a descendant of King James.

On April 11, 1951, the precious Stone of Destiny was stolen. Radical Scottish nationalists who were resentful of English possession of one of Scotland's oldest treasures had committed the crime. This event sparked off a national panic in Great Britain, because without it any future coronation would be technically invalid. An intensive police investigation eventually found the stone 107 days later, hidden at the Scottish abbey of Forfar, Angus. Unfortunately the stone had been split in two during its absence and therefore required careful restoration by experts before its next public engagement, the coronation of Queen Elizabeth II in 1953.

At the turn of the millennium, the stone (weighing 485 lbs.) was returned to Scotland. Its new home is in Edinburgh Castle and it is only to be moved to Westminster on very rare occasions, and then only for the purpose of providing the seat for the coronation of a new British sovereign.

The only argument that can be made against the identification of the stone as one of the Grail Hallows is that the relic is roughly rectangular rather than circular. Its symbolic importance still lies in its role in "king-making." Many early accounts of the inauguration of Celtic kings state that as part of the proceedings, the nobles lifted the new monarch upon a circular shield. This ceremony was last performed in the ruins of Scone Abbey in 1652, when Charles II was proclaimed King of Scots. It is likely that the ideas of the Stone of Destiny and the lifting upon a shield have become garbled with the passage of time. So it may be that it is a dim memory of these rites that has been preserved both in the Grail Stories as the dish and in the Tarot as the suit of Coins.

6

The Minor Arcana of the Tarot

Most books on Tarot cards tend to dwell on the masses of symbolism and meaning contained within the Major Arcana cards. However, the cards of the Minor Arcana have a dazzling complexity of their own. The reason for this apparent neglect may be that, while the Major Arcana cards are filled with strange, exotic and often frightening images, the Minor Arcana cards were until very recently (historically speaking) just a set of Wands, Coins, Swords and Cups in various arrangements according to their numbers. Just like a deck of modern playing cards.

Until A.E. Waite collaborated with Pamela Coleman-Smith to produce the first set of fully illustrated cards, the symbolism of the Minor Arcana was completely concealed. It is extremely probable that Waite did not put much input into the pictorial designs on the numbered cards—that honor belongs to the previously unsung (and shockingly underpaid) Coleman-Smith.

A once popular folk ballad concerning a deck of cards may provide a clue to the original use of the Minor Arcana. During the course of the song, a young soldier is found apparently playing cards during a church service. Threatened with punishment for this blasphemous act by his sergeant, the young man swears that his intentions are pure and explains himself by stating that when he sees the Ace, he is reminded that there is one God. The Deuce reminds him that the Bible is divided into the Old and New Testaments. The Trey is symbolic of Father, Son and Holy Ghost, while the Four represents the Apostles, Matthew, Mark, Luke and John. The Five stands for the five wise virgins who trimmed their lamps, while the Six represents the six days of creation, in which God created the heavens and the earth. The Seven, following on, is the day upon which God rested. The Eight represents the eight righteous people whom God saved during the great flood: Noah, his wife, his three sons and their wives. The Nine represents the nine ungrateful lepers who were cured by Jesus, while the Ten obviously symbolizes the Ten Commandments.

As if this were not enough, the young soldier goes on to state that the King is God himself, the queen is the Blessed Virgin Mary, while the Jack or Knave is the Devil. He then says that there are 365 spots on the deck, the number of days in the year. There are 52 cards, the number of weeks in the year, 4 suits for the seasons, 12 picture cards to stand for the months, and finally, 13 tricks for the number of weeks in a quarter. So, as the ballad states, the deck of cards was at once a Bible, an almanac and a prayer book.

It is likely that if such a wealth of meaning can be gleaned from the modern playing card deck, then its ancestor, the Minor Arcana, contained at least an equal wealth of symbolism. Indeed, it doesn't take too much imagination to connect the four suits with the four classes or divisions of medieval society. The Wands, Rods or Clubs can easily be associated with the mass of the peasantry, the Cups surely represent the clergy, the Coins are obviously tradesmen and merchants, while the regal Swords denote the upper classes, the knights and the nobility.

Compass directions and seasons can also be found within the four suits. Wands are connected to the summer months as well as the hot southerly direction. Cups are autumnal and they also relate to the luxuries of the exotic East. Coins represent winter and cold north, while energetic Swords symbolize new life thrusting from the earth in the springtime, as well as the westerly direction.

As we explore the mysteries of the Minor Arcana, we should be prepared for some surprises, not the least of which is the realization that the Major and Minor cards were not originally intended to be together and that their points of origin are far removed from each other. Whereas the Major cards seem to have a basis in the Qabalah with certain awkward aspects emerging when astrology is added to their symbolism, the Minor Arcana seems to have an astrological base, with the Qabalah being added later.

The Minor Arcana and the Zodiac

The attribution of the cards of the Minor Arcana to the signs and decans of the zodiac is purely a Golden Dawn conception. The notion was probably conceived by one of the order's founders, Samuel Liddell MacGregor Mathers (the same man who applied the Tarot Trumps to the pathways of the Tree of Life). This was a direct result of associating the minor cards to the four traditional elements of Fire, Water, Air and Earth. Wands were identified with Fire, Cups to Water, Swords to Air and Coins to Earth.

As we all know, the zodiac consists of 12 signs, namely Aries the Ram, Taurus the Bull, Gemini the Twins, Cancer the Crab, Leo the Lion, Virgo the Maiden, Libra the Scales, Scorpio the Scorpion, Sagittarius the Archer, Capricorn the Goat, Aquarius the Water-Carrier and Pisces the Fish. These signs are subdivided among the four classical elements so that Aries is a Fire sign, Taurus is governed by Earth, Gemini by Air, Cancer by Water and so on in the same sequence.

Fire	Earth	Air	Water
Wands	Coins	Swords	Cups
Aries	Taurus	Gemini	Cancer
Leo	Virgo	Libra	Scorpio
Sagittarius	Capricorn	Aquarius	Pisces

However, the Golden Dawn did not consider the signs of this familiar form of astrology to be the oldest type of zodiac in existence. We must remember that the members of the mystical order were enamored of the magic and mystery of Ancient Egypt, so they also adopted the system of decans from the civilization of the Nile. To put it simply, a decan consists of ten degrees (a sign of the zodiac being 30 degrees or one twelfth of a circle). So each sign of the zodiac is made up of three decans, making 36 decans in all. So all that remained was to find the right minor card for the right decan.

The first step in this process was to remove the aces from each suit, because it was considered that they represented the purest or archetypal forms of their respective elements. Thus the Ace of Wands was given the esoteric title of "The Root of the Powers of Fire," likewise the Ace of Cups was considered to be "The Root of the Powers of Water" and so on. It is for this reason that the aces do not appear in the zodiac arrangement of the minor cards, but are represented by all three signs of their respective elements.

The Ace of Wands is associated with the three Fire signs of Aries, Leo and Sagittarius. The Ace of Cups is allocated the Water signs of Cancer, Scorpio and Pisces. The Ace of Swords gains the attributes of the Air signs of Gemini, Libra and Aquarius. The Ace of Coins connects with the Earth signs of Taurus, Virgo and Capricorn.

The 16 Court Cards of Page, Knight, Queen and King did not quite fit the scheme either, so these too were removed. The Pages were relegated to symbolizing the four quadrants of the earth, much like the segments of an orange. So, the Page of Wands became associated with the geographical location roughly corresponding to Asia, the watery Page of Cups to the vast Pacific Ocean, the Page of Swords to the Americas and, finally the Page of Coins to Europe and Africa.

The remaining Knights, Queens and Kings were each given a sign of the zodiac corresponding to their respective elements. More details of this are given in sections dealing with the individual cards as well as in a summary later in this book.

With the aces and court cards now removed, we are left with 36 numbered cards, providing a perfect fit for the 36 decans. But the question still remained: Where to start and in what order? Returning to the Golden Dawn's Egyptian inspiration, Mathers reasoned that rather than beginning at the first decan of Aries the Ram—in other words, logically at the beginning of the first sign of the zodiac—he would begin at the start of the Ancient Egyptian cycle. The marker for this was the so-called "Royal Star," which Mathers identified as Cor Leonis or "the Heart of the Lion" in the constellation Leo. As a matter of fact, he was wrong on this point; the true beginning of the Egyptian yearly cycle was Sirius the Dog Star, the brightest star in the heavens, as you will see later.

Nevertheless, for Mathers, Leo rather than Aries became the starting point for the attribution of minor cards to the zodiac. Other prominent members of the Golden Dawn, such as A. E. Waite and W. B. Yeats, did not agree, and insisted that the decan attributions begin at the traditional point, the start of Aries. Their argument eventually won the day.

So after a fierce dispute, the Two of Wands became associated with the first decan of Aries, the three was identified with the second decan, and the four with the third, all being found within the element of Fire. For the five, six and seven of Wands, the three decans of the next Fire sign, Leo were used. Finally the eight, nine and ten were given the three decans of Sagittarius. The same formula was followed for all the remaining minor cards.

Now the problem became: "How to individualize the cards so that they arrive at a coherent divinatory meaning?" To address this problem, Mathers proposed a sequence of the seven astrological planets in the following order: Mars, the Sun, Venus, Mercury, the Moon, Saturn and finally Jupiter. This particular order of the planets is based on a medieval system known as the planetary hours, and, in its original form, it was used to help magicians and those involved in witchcraft invoke suitable powers for their spells. Be that as it may, the order of the planets was then combined with the decan system to provide an individual meaning for each card plus a symbolic title in keeping with that interpretation. It is from these 36 symbolic titles that the modern divinatory interpretations of the cards of the Minor Arcana are derived.

In 1912 the notorious Aleister Crowley, an adept of the Golden Dawn, soon to be dubbed "the wickedest man in the world," added his own interpretations to the planets and decans. He provided many of the minor cards with an alternative title, thereby, in his own view refining the attributions of his great rival, Mathers. So, the Three of Wands, relating to the Sun in Aries, may possess the title "Established Success" or alternatively Crowley's own version of "Virtue." Likewise the Five of Coins, to which Mathers allocated the title "Material Troubles," becomes in Crowley's version, "Worry." Where appropriate, Crowley's card titles are given secondary place in the following table.

The Minor Arcana and the Tree of Life

Having completed the zodiacal attributions of the cards, the adepts of the Golden Dawn turned their attention to the possible Qabalistic symbolism of the Minor Arcana. This, they found, did not fit the minor cards quite as well as it suited the Major Trumps.

Minor Card (excluding Aces and Court Cards)	Planet (in order of planetary hours)	Zodiac Sign & Decan		Symbolic Title(s) (1) Mathers (2) Crowley
Two of Wands	Mars	Aries	1	Dominion
Three of Wands	Sun	Aries	2	(1) Established Success (2) Virtue
Four of Wands	Venus	Aries	3	(1) Perfected Work (2) Completion
Five of Coins	Mercury	Taurus	1	(1) Material Troubles (2) Worry
Six of Coins	Moon	Taurus	2	Material Success
Seven of Coins	Saturn	Taurus	3	(1) Success Unfulfilled (2) Failure
Eight of Swords	Jupiter	Gemini	1	(1) Shortened Force (2) Interference
Nine of Swords	Mars	Gemini	2	(1) Despair (2) Cruelty
Ten of Swords	Sun	Gemini	3	Ruin
Two of Cups	Venus	Cancer	1	Love
Three of Cups	Mercury	Cancer	2	Abundance
Four of Cups	Moon	Cancer	3	(1) Luxury (2) Blended Pleasure
Five of Wands	Saturn	Leo	1	Strife

Six of Wands	Jupiter	Leo	2	Victory
Seven of Wands	Mars	Leo	3	Valor
Eight of Coins	Sun	Virgo	1	Prudence
Nine of Coins	Venus	Virgo	2	Material Gain
Ten of Coins	Mercury	Virgo	3	Wealth
Two of Swords	Moon	Libra	1	Peace Restored
Three of Swords	Saturn	Libra	2	Sorrow
Four of Swords	Jupiter	Libra	3	(1) Truce (2) Rest from Strife
Five of Cups	Mars	Scorpio	1	Disappointment
Six of Cups	Sun	Scorpio	2	Pleasure
Seven of Cups	Venus	Scorpio	3	(1) Illusionary Success (2) Debauch
Eight of Wands	Mercury	Sagittarius	1	Swiftness
Nine of Wands	Moon	Sagittarius	2	Great Strength
Ten of Wands	Saturn	Sagittarius	3	Oppression
Two of Coins	Jupiter	Capricorn	1	Harmonious Change
Three of Coins	Mars	Capricorn	2	Material Works
Four of Coins	Sun	Capricorn	3	Earthly Power
Five of Swords	Venus	Aquarius	1	Defeat
Six of Swords	Mercury	Aquarius	2	(1) Earned Success (2) Science
Seven of Swords	Moon	Aquarius	3	(1) Unstable Effort (2) Futility
Eight of Cups	Saturn	Pisces	1	(1) Abandoned Success
				(2) Indolence
Nine of Cups	Jupiter	Pisces	2	Material Happiness
Ten of Cups	Mars	Pisces	3	(1) Perpetual Success (2) Satiety

This is probably because the two parts of the Tarot had completely different origins—the Minor cards originating in Western Europe (as you can see in the chapter on the Four Grail Hallows) and the Trumps in the hermetically inclined courts of Northern Italy.

Yet again, the Court Cards of each suit had to be ditched. However, Mathers and his compatriots made a valiant effort and decided that the ten numbered cards in each suit could stand for the Sephirot of the Tree of Life, while the Major Cards stood for the pathways between them. The logic was simple; aces being the first cards, could stand for Kether the Crown, the first of the Sephirot.

Twos could be Chockmah, the second, and so on until the most material level of Malkuth is reached with the Ten.

So now each numbered Minor card had the symbolism of a planet, a sign of the zodiac and one of the Qabalistic Sephirot attached to it. This is fertile ground to establish the meanings of the individual cards of the Minor Arcana.

Number Symbolism and the Minor Arcana

Besides all the complex astrological and Qabalistic symbolism that underlies the Minor Arcana, there is also the question of the western tradition of the significance of numbers. The Qabalah is, in essence, a numerological system based on the mysticism of the ancient Hebrews and possibly that of Ancient Egypt itself.

Minor Arcana Card	Sephirot	Symbolizing
Ace	Kether, the Crown	divine glory, light, the first created
Two	Chockmah	wisdom, masculinity, dynamic, positive
Three	Binah	understanding, femininity, potential, compassion
Four	Hesed	love, justice, benevolence
Five	Geburah	power, wrath, violence, cruelty
Six	Tiphareth	beauty, the savior, enlightenment, rebirth
Seven	Netzah	endurance, nature, passion, instinct
Eight	Hod	majesty, intellect, reason, ingenuity
Nine	Yesod	foundation, growth and decay, increase and decrease
Ten	Malkuth	the kingdom, the senses, the material universe

Nevertheless, as previously stated, this esoteric philosophy does not seem quite in tune with the Minor cards. Perhaps the cards are designed to fit another, more "planetary" version of numerology.

If the Minor cards did originate in Western Europe, then the legacy of the Roman Empire in that region would make the Greek version of numerology more familiar than the Hebrew. This version is called the Pythagorean method after Pythagoras, the mathematician and religious leader. Pythagoras and those who followed him endowed each number from one to nine with a mystical significance. The number one became associated with beginnings and creation itself, as in the Qabalistic variant, and was regarded as being solar in nature. However, the number two is not masculine as in Hebrew tradition; it is definitely feminine, yielding, changeable and emotional, and therefore associated with the Moon.

A brief breakdown of Western number symbolism with a short interpretation follows.

Number	Astrological Correspondence	Interpretation
1	The Morning Sun	The Initiator
2	The New or Waning Moon	The Integrator
3	Jupiter	The Achiever
4	The Earth or Setting Sun	The Realist
5	Mercury	The Communicator
6	Venus	The Peacemaker
7	The Full Moon	The Magician
8	Saturn	The Entrepreneur
9	Mars	The Crusader
10	*Returns to the symbolism of 1 because 0 did not exist in ancient Greece or Rome, so it does not count in this system.*	

7

The Suit of Wands

The suit of Wands is variously also known as Rods, Batons, Staves, Sticks, Clubs as in a conventional deck of cards, and very occasionally Scepters. This suit is governed by the element of Fire, and since the Golden Dawn astrological attributions of the cards begin with the Fiery element, this can be regarded as the first of the Tarot suits. Be that as it may, the Wands are related to the Fire signs of astrology, namely Aries, Leo and Sagittarius.

The suit of Wands is said to be one of the masculine suits. Indeed, the symbols are phallic in appearance and the suit as a whole is considered to be very active. The other masculine suit, the suit of Swords, is likewise thought of as having phallic symbols and being equally vigorous.

The Wands suit is associated with effort, and therefore, with work of all kinds. The suit is also connected to the concept of growth, and as a subsidiary association, with communications and negotiations.

The Ace of Wands

***Esoteric Title: The Root of the Powers of Fire
Key Concepts: The start of an enterprise***

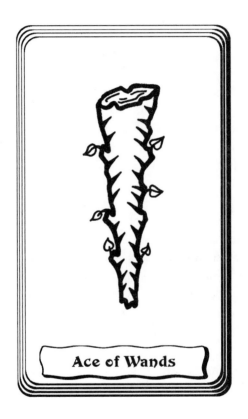

Astrological Relationship:

The Element of Fire, expressing the primal spark of creation and the life force itself. It has been suggested that the Ace of Wands represents a feeble shoot emerging from the earth. Weak and vulnerable, it may be, but within its essence is the potential to become a mighty tree. Another analogy is the first glimmering of flame resulting from the friction caused by rubbing two pieces of wood together.

Tree of Life Position:

Kether, the Crown, the first created sphere of the Tree of Life.

Positive Meaning:

The Ace of Wands can be considered as the first of the aces because it not only begins this suit, but also the entire sequence of the Minor Arcana cards. All aces tend to refer to new beginnings, but none more so than this one, which also indicates initiative, drive, a sense of purpose and the stirring of ambition.

In keeping with the suit's work-related nature, the career is often the area indicated for the card's maximum influence. A new job, a novel enterprise or a stimulating project is shown. A broader view of this ace can indicate the start of life or the birth of a child, as well as the arrival of good news and excellent prospects for your fortunes.

Negative Meaning:

This card does not really have a negative interpretation. It can, however show a delay to your plans, or show that you are not quite as ready to put them into action as you thought you were.

It may reveal that you need someone else's help in the initial stages of a new project, or that you need to tone down your high-flown plans to make them simpler and more workable.

The card sometimes warns against being too single minded or tactless. Even so, the outlook is still good.

The Two of Wands

Esoteric Title: Dominion
Key Concepts: Partnership and positive thinking

Two of Wands

Astrological Relationship:

Mars in Aries. Mars is the ruling planet of Aries, so it is considered "Dignified" when in the sign. All the enthusiastic, energetic, assertive, dominant, masculine features of the red planet are therefore enhanced. This includes more negative traits such as lack of patience, irritability and a confrontational attitude.

Tree of Life Position:
Chockmah, the sphere of wisdom.

Positive Meaning:

The adage "Great oaks from little acorns grow" is particularly apt when considering the Two of Wands. From small beginnings come great things. A meeting of minds, a working partnership and harmonious business dealings are indicated. Promising developments in connection with the working life and with friendships are shown.

This card shows great potential in all areas of life and is particularly beneficial to your interests in regard to property matters.

Negative Meaning:

A clash of personalities and friction within one particular relationship are indicated when the Two of Wands is reversed. Although a working partnership is the most obvious area to be affected, the friction is not necessarily confined to the area of career.

Frustration due to other people's incompetence is shown, as well as troubling issues of trust and pride. An inability to adapt may be the source of the problem.

The Three of Wands

Esoteric Title: Established Success or Virtue
Key Concepts: Good luck and excellent opportunities

Three of Wands

Astrological Relationship:

Sun in Aries. The Sun is always a powerful force, but in Aries it achieves exceptional intensity, being considered "exalted" when in the sign. One prominent influence of this placement is an extreme dislike of complication. Those with the Sun in Aries want a straightforward life, clear communications and transparent motives in others.

Other traits include emotional warmth, enthusiasm and impatience.

Tree of Life Position:
Binah, the sphere of understanding.

Positive Meaning:
This is considered one of the best cards in the Tarot deck. The Three of Wands is a card of good fortune.

However it also shows a period of hard work, of fast and furious activity, and much being crammed into a short space of time. All this is to your benefit because this also signals the start of a period of prosperity. Letters, phone calls, emails, good news and many short journeys increase your chances at this promising time. Partnerships will prosper both in personal and professional terms.

The Three of Wands is a good omen for the establishment of a close relationship such as marriage. Luck is on the way!

Negative Meaning:
This card cannot be too negative, even when reversed. It may show delays, but luck is still with you. It does show a need for extra patience and possibly a need to swallow one's pride in some way. Being too independent at this time is not a good idea, so it is wise to open up to the offers that are being made to you.

The Four of Wands

Esoteric Title: Perfected Work or Completion
Key Concepts: Prosperity, artistic excellence and home life

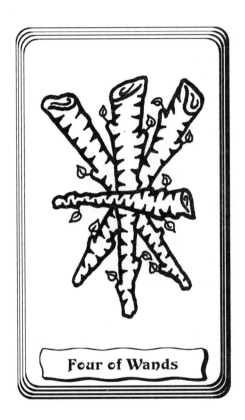

Four of Wands

Astrological Relationship:

Venus in Aries supplies an influence that is creative, lively, passionate and impulsive. The heart is worn on the sleeve when the planet of love is in this Cardinal, Fire sign. However, there is a desire to rule the roost when a relationship has been established.

Tree of Life Position:

Hesed, the sphere of love.

Positive Meaning:

The Four of Wands indicates the successful completion of a project and the satisfaction of a job well done. It is a card of stability and the establishment of something worthwhile.

It sometimes indicates setting up a longed-for home, purchasing new property or, possibly building work or redecoration. The card has artistic associations too, and can reveal success in a creative field, implying recognition of one's talents. The effects of this improvement will be profound in an uplifting sense. They are all positive in nature and will improve your self-image and lifestyle.

Negative Meaning:

The reversed Four of Wands acts something like a straightjacket and reveals uncomfortable feelings of restriction and frustration. You may feel creatively restricted, trapped in a situation of boring, thankless drudgery.

You may feel an inadequacy that fosters despondent moods, but this is the surface situation, because the truth is far more positive than you admit. Good news is on its way. Your fortunes will improve as delays and frustrations gradually fade into the past.

The Five of Wands

Esoteric Title: Strife
Key Concepts: Challenges and competitions

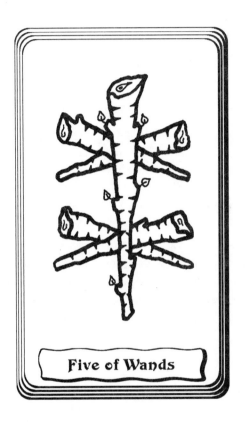

Five of Wands

Astrological Relationship:

Saturn in Leo. There is something of a conflict between the exuberance of Leo and the sobering influence of Saturn. There is certainly a desire for high quality in everything. Nothing second best will do. The determination to achieve this can cause problems, especially when one aims too high and one's target is too implausible. The placement can also indicate pomposity.

Tree of Life Position:
Geburah, the sphere of power.

Positive Meaning:
The Five of Wands indicates a challenge. However, you may not feel adequate to the task before you, so you may also feel insecure and anxious. Take heart, the Five of Wands shows that you are up to the job despite your reservations. You may have to overcome a personal problem such as shyness to take this task on, asserting your presence and authority in a manner you have never attempted before. Overcoming the challenge will give you a tremendous sense of accomplishment.

A subsidiary meaning of the card suggests dealing with written agreements and contractual obligations.

Negative Meaning:
Arguments and bitter disputes can arise over petty matters when the card is reversed. You may be under stress, overly anxious and you may feel somewhat vulnerable and inferior.

Legal and work matters may cause you worry, but you will not necessarily be unsuccessful. However, it would not be wise to be too trusting at this time.

The Six of Wands

Esoteric Title: Victory
Key Concepts: Overcoming the odds, being a winner

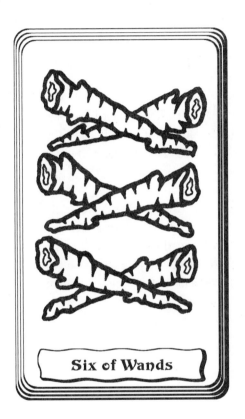

Astrological Relationship:

The placement of Jupiter in Leo is an exuberant, optimistic and creative one. There may be a tendency to bossiness, but there is also genuine leadership ability. Those with this placement think big, manage to do extraordinary things and also to overcome seemingly impossible odds.

Tree of Life Position:

Tiphareth, the sphere of beauty.

Positive Meaning:

After the challenges and the conflict shown in the Five of Wands, the Six represents the victorious aftermath of the battle. The appearance of this card gives you the chance to revel a little in your own triumph, to experience the satisfaction of success. You may take this opportunity to reflect on how hard your struggle has been and to appreciate the fact that you have overcome it.

The card can also indicate business advancement, promotion, a successful negotiation or a legal triumph. There is no doubt that the Six of Wands is a good omen for the future.

Negative Meaning:

Like many other Wands cards, the reversed position of the Six is not necessarily bad. It still promises that you will achieve your desires and win through to your own personal victory, but there may still be a few hurdles in your path. Don't worry, have patience and try not to force the issue. Luck will come to you, albeit in its own time. You will only waste your energies and time if you continue to push for immediate results.

The Seven of Wands

Esoteric Title: Valor
Key Concepts: Defiance and resolute decision

Seven of Wands

Astrological Relationship:

The courageous influence of Mars in Leo gives tremendous self-confidence. The concept of defeat is unknown to this type of person, who will pursue his goals to the end and defend his position with equal vigor. This placement gives leadership qualities and organizational talent.

Tree of Life Position:

Netzah, the sphere of endurance.

Positive Meaning:

Like other odd-numbered Wands cards, the Seven presents a challenge by placing obstacles in your path. However, this does not mean that you will come to a dead halt! The problems around you can be solved with ingenuity and determination. It is best to stand your ground and assert your position forcefully. There may be more than one issue to deal with at once. Be methodical and deal with each in turn. Be brave! Remember that you've faced worse troubles in the past and will overcome this too!

Negative Meaning:

Being prone to self-doubt is the worst headache connected with the reversed Seven of Wands. Even though you could overcome your problems if you approached them the right way, your own timidity could be your biggest problem. However, the outlook is good if you can get a grip on your insecurities.

In addition, an unusual and possibly potentially embarrassing situation could arise, and this would require immediate action to resolve.

The Eight of Wands

Esoteric Title: Swiftness
Key Concepts: Travel, communication and news

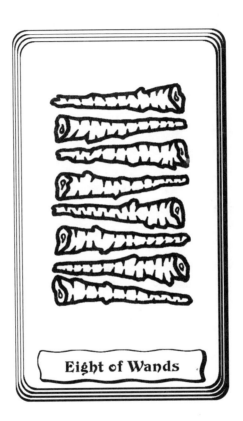

Eight of Wands

Astrological Relationship:

The fast-moving planet Mercury is aptly placed in Sagittarius, the sign of far distant travel. This implies many interests as well as long journeys and versatility, but can also indicate restlessness and impulsive decision-making.

It may also indicate the ability to grasp complex ideas very quickly, as well as subtly gleaning hidden meanings within messages.

Tree of Life Position:

Hod, the sphere of majesty.

Positive Meaning:

Hold onto your hat, because the Eight of Wands signifies a faster pace in all your affairs. You will need to think on your feet, act quickly and perhaps out-talk your opponents now. You will need to be quick-witted and to react immediately to rapidly changing situations.

The card can also indicate travel, but your journeys are likely to be connected to business rather than pleasure. This is a communicative card, so you can expect more phone calls, emails, letters and being bombarded by people who want to share a few words with you.

The Eight of Wands is also said to speed up the events revealed in the other cards of your reading.

Negative Meaning:

The reversed Eight of Wands is very frustrating. Like other reversed Wands, it forecasts delays, unexpected complications, talking at crossed purposes and missed phone calls. People who you need to see become unavailable and your impatience is likely to reach boiling point. You may be rude to someone who you really should not offend. One particular warning associated with the reversed Eight is not to commit your views to writing at this time, because you wouldn't want your private thoughts to become public knowledge.

The Nine of Wands

Esoteric Title: Great Strength
Key Concepts: Resilience, stability and strength

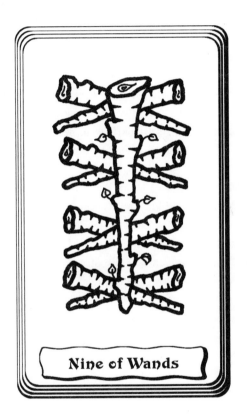

Nine of Wands

Astrological Relationship:

The practical application of learned wisdom is the main attribute of the Moon in Sagittarius. A direct approach will always be preferred to any underhanded schemes. One will always "know where you are" with a person whose natal Moon is found in the sign of the Archer. There are vast emotional resources available to such a person, and he can be very resilient in the face of opposition.

Tree of Life Position:

Yesod, the sphere of foundation.

Positive Meaning:

If you find yourself in a period of stress, then the appearance of the Nine of Wands is extremely reassuring. The card promises that if you stand firm just a little longer, then you will win through all difficulties and achieve the security and stability that you have yearned for. Be patient, wait and maintain your vigilance.

The point is that you are in a place of safety at the moment. You can hold your position because you are unassailable. This card is also good news for your self-confidence, because you will know that you can deal with anything that the world throws at you.

Negative Meaning:

Your opinions are likely to be misguided when this card appears in the reversed position. The stability of the upright Nine is now likely to become obstinate inflexibility. You may refuse to compromise when involved in a dispute, even though this is the only way in which a solution may be found.

The Ten of Wands

Esoteric Title: Oppression
Key Concepts: Heavy burdens, stress and dedication

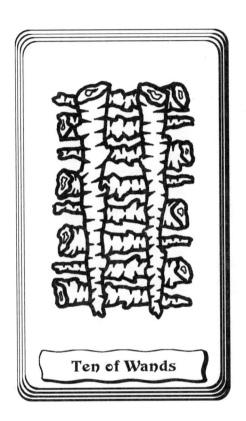

Astrological Relationship:

The gloomy influence of Saturn can dampen the innate enthusiasm of Sagittarius. Saturn implies burdens and hard, thankless work, while Sagittarius longs for freedom and lack of responsibility. On the other hand, the two can work together, combining single-mindedness and strength of purpose with breadth of vision and a sense that all efforts are for some greater purpose.

Tree of Life Position:

Malkuth, the "Kingdom," signifying the material universe.

Positive Meaning:

Even though this card can be regarded as an unwelcome forecast of mammoth effort, it actually does promise considerable success at the end of a difficult process. The Ten of Wands indicates a period of great pressure due to the acceptance of the inevitability of duty and all the hard work that the responsibility entails. You may shoulder burdens, engage in an arduous task or feel that you are under excessive stress.

On the other hand, you have the willpower, the resources and all the determination you could possibly need to carry this obligation through to a worthwhile conclusion. You will find it necessary to prioritize and put a vital task first while deferring less important matters until your have the time and energy to deal with them.

Negative Meaning:

There is very little difference between the upright and reversed meanings of the Ten of Wands. However, when reversed the card shows that other people may place unnecessary pressure upon you and expect you to sort out their problems when you have enough of your own. Watch out for advantage takers—people who have their own agendas that (needless to say) do not include your well-being.

8

The Suit of Coins

This suit is associated with material values and it is also connected to money, goods and possessions. It also throws light on issues such as the questioner's status and what he or she wishes to gain. It is one of the two feminine suits of the Minor Arcana (the other being Cups), and is related to the three astrological Earth signs, Capricorn, Taurus and Virgo, each of which have a direct relationship with three cards of the suit.

The Coin cards are also popularly entitled Pentacles, Disks, Spheres or even Stones. Following the work of A. E. Waite and his Golden Dawn brethren, these cards have usually been called Pentacles. Crowley on the other hand preferred to call them Disks.

In early Italian Tarot decks they were definitely referred to as "Denarii" or "Money" and indeed their divinatory meanings always seem to come back to the "root of all evil" in one way or another. In a conventional deck of cards, the Coins are the Diamonds.

The Ace of Coins

Esoteric Title: The Root of the Powers of Earth
Key Concept: A foundation stone, this ace also expresses
the desire to gain, to own and to possess. Its essence is
extremely materialistic.

Ace of Coins

Astrological Relationship:

The fruitful element of Earth. In the 1930s, Aleister Crowley suggested that the Ace of Coins came under the astrological rulership of the then newly discovered planet Pluto, possibly because the god of the Underworld was considered to grant wealth through mining and the discovery of buried treasure.

Tree of Life Position:

Kether, the Crown. Representing the "Primum mobile," the "First Mover;" in other words, the original source of everything.

Positive Meaning:

This card points to the start of a period of prosperity. It can show good news about cash or money from an unexpected source, such as a windfall payment or through gambling. However, it is more likely that an opportunity will be provided that will lead you to increased wealth. In many illustrations of the card, a path leads off into the distance to a lush garden or a luxurious palace showing that you are about to take the first step on the road to improving your financial position.

Its key concept as a foundation stone indicates that you will soon have a firm base on which to build, and that your life will be entering a phase of stability and steady progress.

Negative Meaning:

When negatively placed, this card reveals an unpleasant picture of financial insecurity. Your foundations are not as solid as you had believed and some drastic action must soon be taken to prevent the loss of money. Greed is also shown here, so take care that you do not make any unsound investments or gamble away your precious resources needlessly.

The Two of Coins

Esoteric Title: Harmonious Change
Key Concepts: Juggling with resources

Two of Coins

Astrological Relationship:

Jupiter in Capricorn. The giant planet in the winter sign of the Goat indicates great resourcefulness and the ability to take on responsibility. Be that as it may, there may be a tendency to be overly careful with small matters while ignoring the larger picture, particularly in career and financial affairs.

Tree of Life Position:

Chockmah, the sphere of wisdom.

Positive Meaning:

In complete contradiction to the esoteric title of the card, the Two of Coins shows hard times, which are often the result of a cash flow crisis. Quite often income will equal expenditure when this card appears. However, your luck has not run out, because with a clever use of your resources, you can meet all your obligations, even if there is nothing left over at the end. The important thing to remember is that you will still be solvent—also, being forced to cope with these difficulties will teach you a great deal.

Negative Meaning:

Recklessness in regard to personal security and finances. Losses through gambling and the inability to meet one's obligations are also likely.

There is also the possibility of a partnership ending. There is a strong sense of desperation when this card is reversed, which is understandable when it becomes obvious that the worst-case scenario here is bankruptcy.

The Three of Coins

Esoteric Title: Material Works
Key Concepts: Skill and accomplishment

Astrological Relationship:

Mars in Capricorn. The aggressive planet Mars promotes ambition and self-reliance. There is an indication of striving to achieve great things, and a total obsession with success. The downside of this position is a tendency to become cold, distant, aloof and somewhat irritable. Wasteful attitudes will rarely if ever be tolerated.

Tree of Life Position:

Binah, the sphere of understanding.

Positive Meaning:

The positive use of your personal skills and talents to forge ahead in the world. The card shows an appreciation of your natural gifts, which leads to profit. One of the nicknames of this card is the "architect," so it also shows building something up for yourself, something that causes you to stand head and shoulders above both friends and enemies alike. Understandably, this remarkable success may cause envious spite from less talented individuals; fortunately, this spite is unlikely to harm you.

The card could possibly indicate a move of home or building improvements in your present property.

Negative Meaning:

Wasting talents and promising opportunities. A refusal to risk a secure and extremely dull situation just in case things could go wrong. Being too conservative in attitude or bowing down to peer-pressure. The message here is to trust in your own abilities!

The Four of Coins

Esoteric Title: Earthly Power
Key Concepts: Material stability and possessions

Astrological Relationship:

Sun in Capricorn. There is a veneer of toughness about the Sun in Capricorn, but this may conceal emotional insecurity. This position indicates a nature that is tenacious, ambitious, somewhat unforgiving and possessing strong opinions.

Tree of Life Position:

Hesed, the sphere of love.

Positive Meaning:

Financial problems will be overcome and you will retain the profits that you have made. This card is often nicknamed "The Miser," but this is generally unfair because the gains, which are so stubbornly held onto, have been hard won and you are entitled to the benefits that they will bring you.

The card also denotes a comfortable lifestyle and brings promise of greater profit in the long term. The only slightly critical aspect of the card is that you might be just a little bit too materialistic at this time.

Negative Meaning:

Delays in the payment of debts, a grasping avaricious mentality, discontent and being envious of the prosperity of others are the less than attractive meanings of this negatively placed card.

To top it all, the reversed Four of Coins may also hint at the failure of exams and other tests unless extra efforts are made.

The Five of Coins

Esoteric Title: Material Troubles
Key Concepts: Poverty, exclusion and hardship

Astrological Relationship:

Mercury in Taurus. The wayward and flighty nature of Mercury is not at home in slow, steady Taurus, indicating that impulsive moves will cause more problems than they will solve. Equally, inflexible attitudes will be counter-productive.

Tree of Life Position:

Geburah, the sphere of power.

Positive Meaning:

This card does not have a very positive meaning, no matter which way up it may be. It denotes hardship, monetary loss and the feeling of being "left in the cold." Helping hands are a rarity at this time, and you may feel dejected and alone. However, all is not as it seems, because help is there to be found, not from someone who is more prosperous than you are, but from someone who is in the same relative position. Be cheerful, there are opportunities to improve your lot. Oddly enough, romance can flourish at this time.

Negative Meaning:

Loss of cash, which could have been avoided if you had paid more attention to paperwork and accounts. You need to reassess your position and move on, and a thorough change in your attitude to money is now vital.

The Six of Coins

Esoteric Title: Material Success
Key Concepts: Generosity, gifts and appreciation

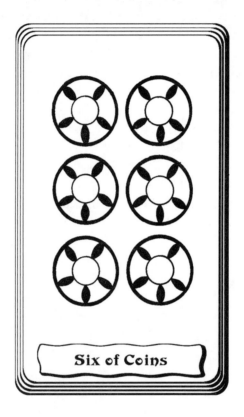

Astrological Relationship:

Moon in Taurus. The changeable Moon is at its most stable in the sign (or decan) of Taurus. This position indicates prosperity as well as financial and emotional support from family and friends. Financial security is vital here, as indeed is the establishment of firm values on which to base decisions.

Tree of Life Position:

Tiphareth, the sphere of beauty.

Positive Meaning:

Money will come to you soon. Other cards should indicate why this is the case. The Six of Coins also shows money being put to good use, and help from someone else. You will be a recipient of a gift or grant and you should therefore be grateful for this benevolence. You might pay off outstanding debts, indulge in pleasurable activities and use your talents to create something new. In fact, you will eventually be in a position to help others in just the same way as you were helped.

Negative Meaning:

Squandering your good fortune. When reversed, the card shows that money will flow out of your hands like water. It can also show the loss of a wallet or purse due to your own carelessness. Other than that, other people could be a constant drain on your resources.

The Seven of Coins

Esoteric Title: Success Unfulfilled
Key Concepts: Planning and steady progress

Seven of Coins

Astrological Relationship:

Saturn in Taurus. The keyword for Saturn is "patience." The ringed planet may provide setbacks, yet in the materialistic sign of Taurus, it indicates that slow, painstaking effort is required to make the best of one's situation.

Tree of Life Position:

Netzah, the sphere of endurance.

Positive Meaning:

Even though the esoteric title of the card is "Success Unfulfilled," it really should be "Success Eventually Fulfilled," because the card points to a time of slow, steady progress which might dampen your spirits but nevertheless will result in great achievements. In other words, do not give up. You definitely are on the right track; just keep at it and the rewards will eventually arrive.

It may also hint at a big project, the very thought of which appears to be overwhelming, saps courage and makes you reluctant to begin. Once you are over this psychological hurdle, you will find that your progress will be easier than you anticipated.

Negative Meaning:

Being discouraged, feeling that you are wasting your efforts, and the firm conviction that you are "going nowhere fast." If you find a task so soul destroying, then perhaps you are involved in the wrong sort of work.

The Eight of Coins

Esoteric Title: Prudence
Key Concepts: Learning and apprenticeship

Eight of Coins

Astrological Relationship:

Sun in Virgo. Application to duty, foresight and practicality are indicated by the sun in the sign or decan of Virgo. This position also indicates a good employee, a diligent servant and a shrewd analyst.

The Sun in Virgo also points to common sense, but there is a tendency to be too fussy and self-critical.

Tree of Life Position:
  Hod, the sphere of majesty.

Positive Meaning:

This is another card of progress, though in this case it has definite implications of education. You will be called upon to patiently learn new skills that will be turned to eventual profit. Work performed now will yield great rewards in the future.

The appearance of this card may herald a new job and gaining qualifications. Even if you do not think that this is the case, you will find that anything you learn at the moment will have relevance to a future career move.

Negative Meaning:

The opposite of patient effort is impatience and the desire to have everything that you want right now.

The reversed card can also mean an enforced period of learning that you will find dull and unrewarding. This may imply that you are dissatisfied with your career or educational course and will have to make a change, even if you find the prospect of change unpleasant or even frightening.

The Nine of Coins

Esoteric Title: Material Gain
Key Concepts: Comfort and prosperity

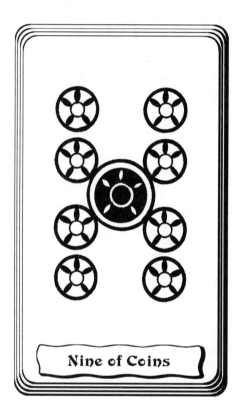

Nine of Coins

Astrological Relationship:

Venus in Virgo. The planet of love is not too comfortable in the sign or decan of the celestial virgin, so there is a hint of disappointment in amorous affairs. On the other hand, business abilities are excellent, as indeed are communication skills. Work in health or beauty fields is favored.

Tree of Life Position:

Yesod, the sphere of foundation.

Positive Meaning:

The Nine of Coins is a card of prosperity. It shows the enjoyment and comfort that money can buy. Obviously, this positive influence indicates a healthy attitude to material resources, because as well as enjoyment, it also implies shrewdness and good sense.

Perhaps relaxation is in order after a period of hard work. So, reward yourself with a treat or two. In a domestic sense, harmony prevails. You may also be inclined to redecorate or to purchase new furniture.

Negative Meaning:

A financial venture that you thought promising will not turn out to be profitable. Heavy debts could be shown or, possibly a life of success and comfort that is based on the misfortunes of others.

The card also indicates a danger of theft or being obliged to sell possessions to make a fast buck in order to get out of a financial scrape.

The Ten of Coins

Esoteric Title: Wealth
Key Concepts: Property, inheritance and family values

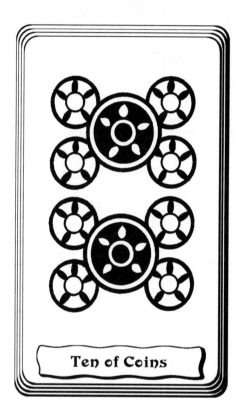

Astrological Relationship:

Mercury in Virgo. Mercury is at its most analytical and practical in the sign or decan of Virgo. Problems are solved with shrewd, precise decisions. Physical well-being and health issues are also highlighted by this position.

Tree of Life Position:

Malkuth, the "Kingdom," the material universe.

Positive Meaning:

As the esoteric title of the card implies, this is a card of great prosperity, not just in material terms but in emotional ones too. It has a strong association with families through the generations, so it may imply inheritance, not just of money and goods, but of traits and positive attitudes too. The card can indicate marriage and the continuance of family traditions.

In business terms, the card shows excellent prospects, especially if there is travel involved. In general though, the "Wealth" of the title means more than just money, though there will be plenty of that; it also points to a spiritual wealth and great happiness.

Negative Meaning:

Family disputes, especially if these are over money or inheritance rights. It can also indicate a tradition that has had its day and is now only serving to stifle future prospects. In this sense, the reversed Ten of Coins can be an indicator of divorce and the resultant division of property and resources.

The Curse of Scotland

The only card of the Coins suit to possess an individual superstition is the nine. In terms of playing cards, this is the Nine of Diamonds, which is known as the "Curse of Scotland" even though its divinatory meaning is positive, implying comfort and prosperity.

Various explanations have been given for this dire title, which was first recorded in the eighteenth century. It has been suggested that the back of the card was used to convey disastrous orders on the field of battle. King James IV is said to have sketched the fatal disposition of his forces before the terrible Battle of Flodden in 1513. Likewise the English commander at the equally appalling Battle of Culloden (1746), "Butcher" Cumberland, is said to have done the same, as indeed did the bloodthirsty Earl of Stair before the Glencoe Massacre in 1692. The fact that this particular Earl used a heraldic shield bearing nine red lozenges may be the origin of this story.

Another tragic figure of Scottish history is also associated with the Nine of Diamonds; this of course is Mary Queen of Scots, who introduced sophisticated card games from the decadent court of France to her puritanical Northern Kingdom. She is also said to have drawn the fateful card on the night before her execution.

The Nine of Diamonds was also nicknamed "The Pope" in a once popular game called "Pope Joan." This Catholic title was hardly likely to warm the hearts of the strictly protestant Scots at a time of religious ferment.

A more prosaic explanation may be that the word "curse" is actually a corruption of "cross" since the diamonds on the card were often arranged in a "saltire," the pattern of St. Andrew's Cross, the flag of Scotland.

9

The Suit of Swords

The Swords suit is airy in nature; it is related to intellectual and mental processes and also with troubles of many kinds. When there is a preponderance of Sword cards in any reading, then you can be sure that difficult times are on their way. However, the answer to any Sword problem can usually be found with an exercise of logic, coolness and a willingness to learn from even the hardest of lessons. Sword cards discriminate; they separate the good from the bad.

It should never be forgotten that Swords are weapons of war. Their appearance implies battles of one sort or another. They are dual edged, having a function that can harm or provide protection. Courage and fortitude are required to face the challenges symbolized by the suit of Swords.

The Swords are the second of the masculine suits, the other being Wands. These sharp, thrusting cards are related to the three Air signs of astrology, Libra, Aquarius and Gemini. In a conventional pack of playing cards, the Swords are the Spades. This name is derived from an Italian word that literally means "sword."

The Ace of Swords

Esoteric Title: The Root of the Powers of Air
Key Concepts: Unstoppable force. The blade of this sword
can cut through anything.

Ace of Swords

Astrological Relationship:

The Element of Air. This element is literally as changeable as the wind. It is intellectual in nature and hints at the constant turmoil of the mind. In Tarot terms, Swords are associated with strife both in terms of physical struggle and intellectual and verbal challenges.

Tree of Life Position:

Kether, the Crown, the first created sphere of the Tree of Life.

Positive Meaning:

This card foretells swift, irrevocable and dramatic changes in your life, probably as the result of your own decisions and actions. Its basic meaning is that of unstoppable force, cutting through all obstacles and winning through to personal victory. When this Sword appears, you can be certain that you have the personal strength, character and determination to defeat any who dare to challenge you, by the sheer force of your willpower!

However, nothing comes without a cost, and in this case, you may have to be prepared to make certain sacrifices in order to fulfill your desires. This is a Sword that has a double blade and cuts both ways. You will find yourself changed as much as your circumstances by the time these events are played out.

Negative Meaning:

Harsh words, arguments and delays are to be expected when this Ace is reversed. The Sword now points at you and you are likely to be wounded in some way. Probably by misunderstandings and the blind prejudices of those who should know better. You may feel that your hopes will be dashed, even though you have a good chance of success. All this leads to anxiety and stress.

You may also become rather tyrannical and sarcastic. Try to remain calm and reasonable at all times.

The Two of Swords

Esoteric Title: Peace Restored
Key Concepts: Balance, equally opposing forces

Astrological Relationship:

Moon in Libra. The ever-changing moon in the balanced sign of Libra suggests that a sense of harmony is so important that it must be maintained at any cost.

It can also indicate that even an uncomfortable status quo continues through an inability to make a decision.

Tree of Life Position:
Chockmah, the sphere of wisdom.

Positive Meaning:
This card can indicate a breathing space in a time of struggle. A decision has to be made or a course of action taken, but as yet there are no clues as to the best thing to do. The most telling image associated with this card is that of two equally matched duelists who circle each other, each looking for an opening that will give him an advantage. Skill and a fair degree of fancy footwork are implied by this image, yet there is no result to all of these wary efforts. The Two of Swords can therefore, indicate a stalemate situation, possibly with acrimonious words.

A peace of sorts is achieved, but this is more in the nature of an armed truce with both sides eyeing each other distrustfully. As with most formal duels, there is moral support available from friends in both camps.

Negative Meaning:
The intricate footwork of the duel is again a feature when this card is negative. However, one or other participant is starting to falter and lose concentration. On the same theme, indecision and a failure to act when opportunity beckons is also likely.

There is also a hint that betrayal is in the offing. Beware of trickery and fraud.

The Three of Swords

Esoteric Title: Sorrow
Key Concepts: Heartache, heartbreak and "cutting away"

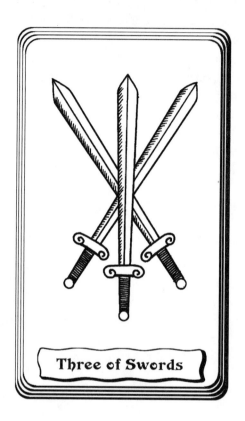

Three of Swords

Astrological Relationship:

Saturn in Libra. Saturn, the grimmest of the seven ancient planets is considered to be "exalted" in Libra and therefore very powerful indeed. The emphasis here is on absolute truth at whatever cost. What makes this process particularly difficult is that Libra is a sign prone to romantic fantasy, but the ruthless, uncompromising nature of Saturn confirms loyalty to a principle, even at the cost of personal relationships.

Tree of Life Position:
Binah, the sphere of understanding.

Positive Meaning:
The appearance of the Three of Swords signals a reality check! Harsh facts have to be faced, because this is a hurtful and uncompromising card. Many interpretations of this card dwell on the possibility that it indicates the irrevocable break up of a relationship, and the subsequent soul searching and readjustment that must take place.

A relationship triangle is sometimes hinted at, in which heartache is inevitable for one participant or for all.

This card is equally likely to reveal illness and may even indicate a surgical operation. Usually this operation will be minor in nature, but nevertheless totally necessary. In either case, that which has been a problem will be irrevocably removed.

Negative Meaning:
This is, on balance, the better position for the card, even though it is still stressful. There may still be a period of upheaval, confusion and worry, yet the healing process has begun, even if there is still a long way to go. Have faith, because the dark clouds will eventually lift.

The Four of Swords

*Esoteric Title: **Truce or Rest From Strife** (from the seventeenth century this card was known as "The Devil's Bedposts.")*
Key Concepts: Recuperation and formulating strategies

Four of Swords

Astrological Relationship:

Jupiter in Libra. Philosophy and spirituality are important concepts connected with certain aspects of Jupiter. Here these ideals are intimately connected with interpersonal relationships as well. The lonely path of spiritual awakening is here associated with social interactions. Being lonely in a crowd perhaps?

Tree of Life Position:
Hesed, the sphere of love.

Positive Meaning:
After a time of struggle, there is a need to retreat from the fray and to take a rest from the ongoing pressures of the world. This card often reveals a period of relative quiet, during which you can put your thoughts in order and formulate a strategy for the future. Removing yourself from a stressful situation will help you to put matters into perspective and to weigh-up the relative importance of those things that are worrying you.

In some cases, the Four of Swords can literally show recuperation from a physical illness or trauma. On the other hand, you may find yourself in attendance on someone else who happens to be ill. Visits to hospital are often quoted as a traditional meaning for the card.

Negative Meaning:
The gloomy side of the card is now emphasized with illness, exile and forced confinement prominent in its interpretation. Dark thoughts and depressive attitudes are also likely. Possibly nervous exhaustion enforces complete rest.

As if this were not bad enough, some sources state that attendance at a funeral will soon follow the appearance of the negative Four of Swords.

The Five of Swords

Esoteric Title: Defeat
Key Concepts: Loss, defeat and obstinacy

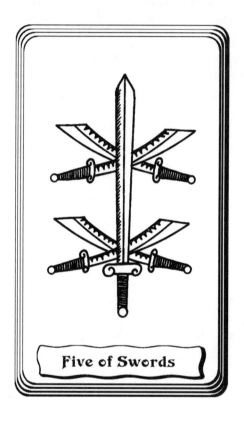

Astrological Relationship:

Venus in Aquarius. The planet of love in the high-minded sign of the water-carrier can promote both popularity and an unfortunate desire to believe romantic fairy-tales, with all the consequent upset and feelings of emotional betrayal. Frequent changes in fortune are also associated with Venus in this sign.

Tree of Life Position:
Geburah, the sphere of power.

Positive Meaning:
Uncontrolled anger and frustrations are major features of this unfortunate card. As its esoteric title suggests, the Five of Swords reveals that the "Game is up." A particular situation has become untenable. Battles fought to rectify the situation are doomed to failure. The sensible option is to turn your back on these circumstances and start over with something else. Unfortunately, a cool head is not part of the card's interpretation, so it is likely that you will persist in trying to overcome impossible odds and refuse to accept your own personal defeat in this matter. However, the defeat will become plain in time and cause genuine suffering. When this card appears, it is definitely time to cut your losses and to get out while your self-respect is intact.

Negative Meaning:
There is little difference between the positive and negative meanings of this card, except that this is one of those occasions when the more "negative" view can, to some extent, actually work in your favor. At least you will find it easier to remove yourself from suffering when the card is in this position.

The Six of Swords

Esoteric Title: Earned Success or Science
Key Concepts: Travel, escape from difficulty, flight

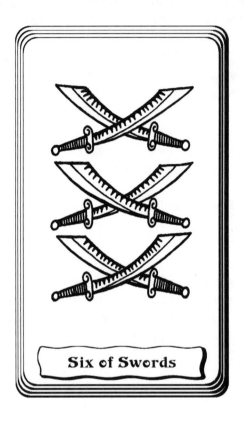

Six of Swords

Astrological Relationship:

Mercury in Aquarius. Mercury, planet of the mind is perfectly at home in the cool, idealistic sign of Aquarius. Although problems remain (as with all the other Sword cards), there is the ability to rationalize one's worries and to examine them in a clear way, hopefully arriving at a successful resolution.

Tree of Life Position:
> Tiphareth, the sphere of beauty.

Positive Meaning:

After the terrible battles of the Five of Swords, it is a relief to find that the Six of Swords is one of the more hopeful cards in this troublesome suit. It means turning your back on strife and heading off for pastures new. This can be taken literally, as a physical escape, but it can also be interpreted in a metaphorical fashion as a change of attitude or an injection of cool reason into a fraught and highly charged situation, enabling you to distance yourself mentally and emotionally.

This is the card that used to be interpreted as "crossing water," again reflecting a hint of an escape from confinement and therefore it may be an indication of travel (especially in company). When the Six of Swords appears, your immediate problems will be solved, but remember that "discretion is the better part of valor!"

Negative Meaning:

The outlook is still good when this card is negative, even though there may be delays and petty problems. The concept of escape and travel holds true here too, but you may be unsure as to your destination.

The Seven of Swords

Esoteric Title: Unstable Effort or Futility (This card has also been nicknamed "the Thief)
Key Concepts: Dishonesty, lies, theft and insecurity

Seven of Swords

Astrological Relationship:

Moon in Aquarius. The deep emotions associated with the moon are curiously muted when in Aquarius. There is a cool detachment, possibly an unfeeling nature. The association with night is also a feature in this card of dishonesty and deception. With this card, what you see is definitely not what you get!

Tree of Life Position:
Netzah, the sphere of endurance.

Positive Meaning:
The Seven of Swords is a difficult card to interpret. It has three distinct connotations. The first is suggested by the esoteric title "Unstable Effort," so it can refer to a period when short periods of frantic activity are interspersed with times when nothing seems to happen at all.

A more sinister interpretation indicates a theft or fraud, so when this card appears, it is important to take extra care of your possessions and pay more attention to home security. On the other hand, the card can show that someone has been "robbed" of confidence by a false friend or a callous lover.

Often, there is indicated a time of intrigue and falsehood, so you must match an opponent in cunning and be prepared to make sacrifices to overcome these difficulties. This card is not favorable to legal affairs and business dealings.

Negative Meaning:
Theft, lies and dishonesty are even more likely when the Seven of Swords is negative. You may meet with malice and deliberate deception. Be even more aware that your property is at risk.

Dealings with contracts or the law will not be to your advantage.

The Eight of Swords

Esoteric Title: Shortened Force or Interference
Key Concepts: Restriction, powerlessness

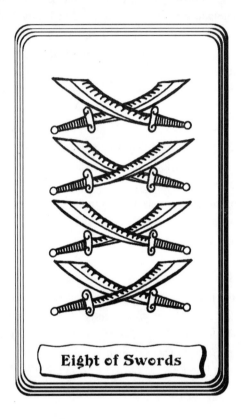

Astrological Relationship:

Jupiter in Gemini. Jupiter is described as being in "detriment" when in the sign of the Twins, so the freedom-loving nature of the planet is therefore restricted and trapped when here. Intellectual pursuits are indicated, but they are likely to be somewhat lacking in scope. This is a frustrating and difficult placement.

Tree of Life Position:
Hod, the sphere of majesty.

Positive Meaning:
There is no doubt that the entire suit of Swords is a troublesome one, and true to form, the Eight is no exception. A run of bad luck is indicated here. It is likely that you will feel trapped in some way by circumstances that are beyond your control. You may be perfectly aware of what is likely to happen next, but will be incapable of taking any action of prevent it. The message here is "Don't panic!" It will not help! Only patient effort will get you out of this quagmire.

On the other hand, the intellectual nature of the Swords suit does suggest a solution. There is likely to be help available to you, if you know where to look for it. It may be that pride stands in the way of asking for assistance—and if that is so, then prepare to eat some humble pie. Be rational and ask!

Negative Meaning:
The frustrations indicated by this card are emphasized now, so they may become almost unbearable. You may be so irritable that you take your negativity out on innocent bystanders—or even worse, on those who would help you.

This is an indicator of someone who is his own worst enemy, probably due to misplaced pride.

The Nine of Swords

Esoteric Title: Despair and Cruelty
Key Concepts: Anxiety, illness and depression

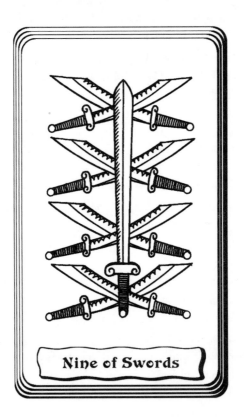

Nine of Swords

Astrological Relationship:

Mars in Gemini. There is an instinctual fear of being trapped with Mars in Gemini. Impulsiveness and a refusal to be restricted by other people's expectations are also features. Mars can be associated with violence and the turmoil of the mind becomes more aggressive and angry when Mars is in Gemini.

Tree of Life Position:

Yesod, the sphere of foundation.

Positive Meaning:

The esoteric title of this card, "Despair and Cruelty," is somewhat misleading, because rather than indicating the unkindness of someone else, it usually means harm inflicted on oneself. It is true that you may be the victim of spite, but it is your own reaction to this malice that causes problems. The Nine of Swords usually shows a period of anxiety, sleepless nights or conversely disturbed dreams added to which is a general feeling of powerlessness and uselessness. In short, these are symptoms of depression. On the other hand, guilt and this enduring form of self-punishment may afflict you.

The card may indicate illness and very low physical and mental reserves. This is particularly relevant to female health problems, the recovery stage of which is likely to be a long, drawn-out process. Whatever the cause of this malaise, it will require a lot of determination for you to come through this dark period intact.

Negative Meaning:

The meaning of the reversed card is little different from the upright meaning. It becomes more likely that your suffering is due to some form of self-punishment or guilt feelings.

You may think your situation is hopeless, which means that you refuse help when it is offered, but the fact is that the opposite is the case and that your period of torment is almost at an end.

The Ten of Swords

Esoteric Title: Ruin
Key Concepts: Betrayal, the lowest point of fortune

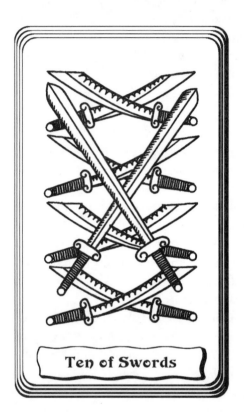

Astrological Relationship:

Sun in Gemini. On the surface, there is little connection between the astrological interpretation of the Sun in Gemini and the card meaning. The sociable, chatty, versatile nature of solar Geminis is not reflected in the harsh meaning of this, the "worst card in the deck."

However, in addition to the "sunny," fun-loving disposition, the dual nature of the sign dictates that there is also a far darker aspect.

If the negative side of the Sun in Gemini is considered, then falsehood and loneliness could be considered as a justification for this placement. On the other hand, the solar influence could indicate a turning point of fortune for the better.

Tree of Life Position:
Malkuth, the "Kingdom," signifying the material universe.

Positive Meaning:
There is a consensus of opinion that the Ten of Swords is the very worst card in the deck. After all, it is the ultimate number card of the most difficult suit. The card's esoteric title "Ruin" speaks for itself. The Ten is an indicator of the lowest point in fortune. When this card turns up in a reading then all that one dreads becomes far more likely. Betrayal, being "stabbed in the back," loss and being left out in the cold being some of the more restrained interpretations.

Nevertheless, this card is associated with dual-natured Gemini, so inevitably there is another way of looking at it! After all, when one's fortunes cannot sink any further the only way is up! When all is lost, what more is there to lose? This is the turning point of fortune, and the long, slow climb back is about to begin. Have courage!

Negative Meaning:
The negative interpretation of the Ten of Swords echoes the basic meaning. Unfortunately, you have not quite reached rock bottom yet. There are still a few more trials to go before you get to the lowest point of your fortune.

Do not give in to despair, your tribulations will soon be over and the recovery process can then begin. Bolster your confidence and lift your mood in any way that you can.

10

The Suit of Cups

The suit of Cups is associated with the depths of the emotions. Romance is to be found here, as well as marriage, close relationships and affections of all kinds. Prosperity too is connected with the Cup cards, though this tends not to refer to finance but to personal comfort and contentment.

Happy feelings are not the only emotions that human beings can experience; within the suit of Cups are found other equally strong, and rather turbulent affairs of the heart. Creative passion may be found here, and the visual arts and music have a particular resonance with the Cup cards.

The suit of Cups may also be called Chalices or Cauldrons. It is a feminine suit, the other being Coins. The suit is related to the Water signs of astrology, Cancer, Scorpio and Pisces. In a conventional deck of cards the Cups are the Hearts, a fact that is quite in keeping with their highly emotional nature.

The Ace of Cups

Esoteric Title: The Root of the Powers of Water
Key Concepts: Outpouring of emotions and artistic
inspiration, the beginning of love

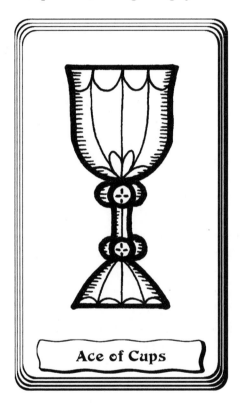

Astrological Relationship:

The element of Water as well as the inspiration provided by the planet Neptune and the subtle, intuitive influence of the Moon. The waxing and waning of the Moon hint at the ebb and flow of the emotions. Neptune presides over artistry, music and mysticism of a mediumistic and psychic kind. It is said that "still waters run deep" and this is the case with the boundless affection, sympathy and kindness associated with the Ace of Cups.

Tree of Life Position:

Kether, the Crown, the first of the spheres of the Tree of Life, from which all others flow.

Positive Meaning:

As with the other aces, the Ace of Cups hints at a beginning, in this case the start of love. The power of the Water element will sweep you along to happiness. Love affairs, betrothals, marriages and births are all likely interpretations of this joyful card. This may symbolize the commencement of a period of inspired creativity that will be nurtured by kindness, understanding, good companionship and happy, emotionally fulfilling events. The appearance of the Ace of Cups ensures that a light heart, emotional contentment, the expression of talent and a gladness to be alive prevail.

Negative Meaning:

Emotions could be racing out of control when this ace is found in the negative position. Exhaustion, disappointments in love and bitter feelings are quite likely at this time.

The negative Ace of Cups could indicate disenchantment and lack of trust with a relationship, stresses within a partnership or unreal expectations in love.

It could equally show a lack of inspiration and as a consequence, a depressive frame of mind.

The Two of Cups

Esoteric Title: Love
Key Concept: Commitment

Astrological Relationship:

Venus in Cancer. The nature of Venus in the sign of Cancer is intuitive and sympathetic. One who is influenced by this placement often turns to loved ones for emotional support. The imagination is extremely strong, as are the instincts, sometimes to the extent of psychic awareness. Venus in Cancer also suggests a love of home comforts.

Tree of Life Position:
Chockmah, the sphere of wisdom.

Positive Meaning:
The primary meaning of this card is love and complete understanding between two people. One could say that it is a meeting of hearts and minds. This card certainly implies emotional contentment and a sense of commitment.

If a deeply emotional interpretation is not apt to the situation, the card can show co-operation, friendship, alliances and mutual respect. It is a good card to get if there have been troubles, because it indicates that bad times are over and harmony will now reign.

Negative Meaning:
The usual negative interpretation of the Two of Cups is that of divorce, separation and infidelity. Even if one does not go that far, there are definitely stresses and strains within a relationship when the card appears in this position. Disappointment and betrayal are a possibility, but the outlook is not completely black.

It is rare that this card indicates irreparable harm or that any separation will be permanent. It merely shows that a few rough times are ahead. Keep your faith!

The Three of Cups

Esoteric Title: Abundance
Key Concepts: Celebrations, marriages and births

Astrological Relationship:

Mercury in Cancer. The intellectual nature of Mercury increases the powers of recall when it is found in the sign of Cancer. The intuition is also boosted, but a person with this influence may become opinionated and obsessive. The fickle side of Mercury may also be evident in affairs of the heart, leading to easy promises being made and also promiscuity.

Tree of Life Position:

Binah, the sphere of understanding.

Positive Meaning:

This is a card of celebration, laughter, fun, parties, flirtation and happy meetings. Marriages, longed-for pregnancies, a birth or the attendance of a christening are traditionally foretold when the Three of Cups appears.

Reunions with family members and old friends are subsidiary meanings too.

Ills are healed; old enmities put to rest and a renewed sense of peace and harmony achieved with this card. In short, the Three of Cups indicates a time when the troubles of the world recede in importance and you can indulge in a measure of carefree fun.

Negative Meaning:

The Three of Cups has a darker, more dangerously self-indulgent side when negative. At the very least, it implies taking the feelings of another for granted. It may show that lust and unwise passions have taken a grip and common sense flown. Promiscuity or the "eternal triangle" in love affairs might also be shown.

Another possibility is that a one-sided love affair exists with affections given but not returned.

Unwelcome news of a marriage or pregnancy might also feature when this card is reversed.

The Four of Cups

Esoteric Titles: Blended Pleasure or Luxury
Key Concepts: Boredom and dissatisfaction

Astrological Relationship:

Moon in Cancer. The Moon is the ruler of Cancer and said to be "dignified" in this sign. Consequently, the lunar influence is very powerful indeed. Intuitive, sensitive and quite moody, the Moon here suggests a home-loving, clannish nature that is possessive of loved ones. It also adds to the kindness and sympathies. A person with the Moon in Cancer tends to be maternal, protective and caring.

Tree of Life Position:
Hesed, the sphere of love.

Positive Meaning:
Discontent is a major theme of this card. Although you may have achieved a certain level of emotional stability, there will be an underlying suspicion that "the grass is greener on the other side of the fence." If only you could find out where this marvelous new lawn is! You may be bored with your life circumstances and long for a change.

In relationship matters especially, this card shows the need for some added excitement, a renewal of romance before it fades away for good. In short, there is a deep emotional yearning for some unidentified "something" when this card appears.

Negative Meaning:
The meaning of this card does not really vary whether its position is upright or reversed, although when reversed, the desperate yearning reaches an extreme. The card may indicate a fear of loneliness or it can denote indulging in pointless pleasure-seeking to stave off boredom.

This is the time when you have to be decisive, no matter how hard that seems. Make a decision, any decision. Make your choice and go for it! After all, it will be better than the emotional void that you currently occupy.

The Five of Cups

Esoteric Title: Disappointment
Key Concepts: Emotional loss, worry and sorrow

Five of Cups

Astrological Relationship:

Mars in Scorpio. Mars is the traditional ruling planet of the sign of the scorpion. The planet's aggressive, passionate nature is therefore strongly emphasized. There may also be tendencies to ruthlessness and secrecy. Self-discipline could be a problem, as well as a tendency to dwell on the past and plot elaborate revenges.

Tree of Life Position:
Geburah, the sphere of power.

Positive Meaning:
In many decks of Tarot cards the Five of Cups shows that three cups remain standing while two are overturned, spilling a liquid reminiscent of blood. When this card appears, there is a sense of irrevocable loss and the consequent emotional distress. It is likely that fond affection has soured, bringing feelings of alienation and hostility into a relationship. Indeed, things may never be quite the same again.

The card is not all bad news, but it does present a challenge. The spilled liquid gives the clue. The proverb "stop crying over spilt milk" has a particular resonance to this card. Put past hurt behind you, and turn your attention to what remains. This may be your chance to leave a situation that has given you little happiness and to strike out in a different, more satisfying direction.

Negative Meaning:
Although the basic meaning of disappointment is the same when this card is reversed, you will find it easier to cope because you will gain far more than you have lost. Any unhappiness will be transitory and it will soon end.

The Six of Cups

Esoteric Title: Pleasure
Key Concepts: Memories, nostalgia and childhood

Astrological Relationship:

Sun in Scorpio. Loyalty to family, friends and colleagues is the main characteristic of the Sun in the sign of Scorpio. A person with this influence makes an excellent friend but a very bad enemy. The influence of Scorpio also promotes strong likes and dislikes. Scorpio is also related to the depths. Its modern ruling planet is considered to be Pluto, the lord of the underworld. This hints at deep psychological roots stretching back to childhood experiences.

Tree of Life Position:
Tiphareth, the sphere of beauty.

Positive Meaning:
The influence of the past and one's own nostalgic attitudes are the main themes of the Six of Cups. In particular, the card relates to childhood and the experiences that have been character forming in the far distant past. Happy memories are emphasized and some links with your background and past in general are likely to resurface.

When this card appears it is also likely that a certain person may come back into your life after a long absence. If this card occurs when you are troubled by any sort of problem (not necessarily emotional in nature), then the answer to the conundrum will be found in your past experience. Look back to similar circumstances, either in your own life or events that occurred elsewhere in your family. Events and decisions made then will provide you with the answer you seek.

Negative Meaning:
The past is a great place to visit, but it is a poor place in which to live! Somehow wish-fulfilling fantasies have intruded on memory when this card is reversed. You may have a rose-tinted view of the past that is obscuring the truth. It is also likely that you are held back by old ideas and the imagined disapproval of childhood role models. Look to the future and do not let the past rule your life.

The Seven of Cups

Esoteric Titles: Illusionary Success or Debauch
Key Concepts: Choices, many opportunities for good or ill

Astrological Relationship:

Venus in Scorpio. The scorpion takes on a softer ambience in the presence of Venus, with a mingling of sensuality and passion. However the obsessive nature of the sign can easily turn this into debauchery and lust.

There may also be a manipulative and possessive tendency to add to the seductive mix. As usual, Scorpio tends to extremes. In this case, either total love or implacable hatred.

Tree of Life Position:
Netzah, the sphere of endurance.

Positive Meaning:
When this card appears, there are some truly amazing opportunities around. However it is up to you to spot them! This is because there are likely to be some dead ends as well! The trouble is that doorways of opportunity are two a penny at the moment, lots of well meaning advice will be given, but none of this will help you to make up your mind. All is not as it seems, so there is little you can rely on. The answer to this problem is to trust your instincts. Reject all advice and do what feels right for you.

Traditional Tarot reading also suggests that if a love affair has been troubled, especially by financial problems, then this will be resolved soon. Both Mathers and Crowley tend to emphasize the negative aspects of this card, quoting the likelihood of making errors of judgment, or an inability to retain the success that has been gained through good decision-making.

Negative Meaning:
The meaning of the reversed Seven of Cups is basically the same as the upright version, with the possibility that wishful thinking may be leading you astray.

Mathers and Crowley do not list reversed meanings, but state that if the card is "negatively aspected," drunkenness, lust, selfish dissipation and wrath are among its connotations; as well as deception in love and friendship.

The Eight of Cups

Esoteric Titles: *Abandoned Success or Indolence*
Key Concepts: *Searching, a quest for fulfillment*

Eight of Cups

Astrological Relationship:

Saturn in Pisces. Although Saturn generally indicates hard work, in the sign of Pisces it promotes idealism and imagination. The dreamy nature of Pisces tends to forget practicalities and the presence of the gloomy ringed planet here can cause self-undoing through over-emotionalism and a lack of grasp on reality.

Tree of Life Position:
Hod, the sphere of majesty.

Positive Meaning:
As the esoteric title suggests, there is a readiness to abandon those things that made one emotionally happy once, and move on in search of better. A break with the past is forecast and it is time to move on and experience the new.

This card is often taken as an omen of pleasurable travel, because it indicates a chance to see more of the world and learn more about yourself while on your journey. Of course, this voyage of discovery need not be a physical one but may show that a spiritual journey of discovery is in store.

If you have been embroiled in other people's petty concerns and have lost sight of your own path, this is a good card to get, because good fortune smiles on you. The message is to follow your heart, because who knows where it could lead you?

Negative Meaning:
Refusing to face up to realities and generally running away from problems. You may be off in pursuit of a fantasy at the expense of all that is worthwhile in your life. The reversed Eight of Cups warns against making far-reaching errors of judgment.

The Nine of Cups

Esoteric Title: Happiness
Key Concepts: Pleasure, fun and frivolity

Astrological Relationship:

Jupiter in Pisces. Jupiter was considered to be the ancient ruler of Pisces and is therefore very powerful in the sign or decan. The optimistic influence of the giant planet promotes imagination, artistic gifts, humanitarianism, generosity and romance. The planet is also an indicator of prosperity, fun and a joyful attitude.

Tree of Life Position:
Yesod, the sphere of foundation.

Positive Meaning:
The esoteric title of this card is "Happiness" and that, in short, is an excellent summary of its meaning. When the Nine of Cups appears in a reading, you can expect great joy to come your way. Your popularity will become evident and your social life in particular will benefit, because there are likely to be celebrations, parties and plenty of visits to places of entertainment.

New people are likely to come into your life and you will find yourself surrounded by many new friends. There is a sense of fun about this card, and the Nine of Cups also suggests improvements in health and in mental attitudes. When this happy card appears, open your heart and mind to new ideas and experiences.

Negative Meaning:
Vanity, arrogance and taking the feelings of others for granted are indicated. Your partner and close friends may feel neglected while you become self-obsessed and fickle in your favors.

On the other hand, the card may show possessiveness on your part, combined with a cloying, overly sentimental show of affection.

The Ten of Cups

Esoteric Titles: Perpetual Success or Satiety
Key Concepts: Contentment and lasting happiness

Ten of Cups

Astrological Relationship:

Mars in Pisces. The relentless drive of Mars turns inward or disappears altogether when the red planet is found in the sign of Pisces. The emotions are the ruling factor and the presence of Mars here suggests that the need for strife has passed—for now at least. The mood of this placement is gentle, artistic and intuitive. It may indicate self-sacrifice for the greater good.

Tree of Life Position:

Malkuth, the material universe.

Positive Meaning:

The Ten of Cups promises peace and prosperity. It is primarily a card of happiness that foretells of a time when your life will be filled with joy. Not only that, but the glorious period indicated by the Ten is going to endure. After all, the esoteric title of the card is "Perpetual Success." The card shows that a wish is about to be fulfilled and everything will work out in the best possible manner.

Your relationships, both those of a romantic nature and those with close friends are set to become more satisfying. The Ten of Cups also has strong associations with family life and domestic harmony.

Negative Meaning:

Even when it is in the reversed position, the Ten of Cups cannot be considered to be a "bad" card. Good fortune still occurs, even though the knocks you may have received will tend to make you rather distrustful of your luck.

It is true that some of your close associates could leave your circle, but new ones are about to be found to fill the gap in your life.

11

The Court Cards—The Suit of Wands

The King and Queen of Wands normally represent people in a reading. In this case, people who may act as advisors, teachers or people with whom one has dealings in business and in daily life.

The Knight and Page can represent people or situations; in situations, these Wand cards often suggest communication or movement in one's affairs, and the need to take action.

Note: Although the illustrations on your cards may show the Pages as male figures, these cards can refer to either sex. I have used the masculine "he" and "him" here to avoid clumsiness, but do bear in mind that these cards are not gender specific. In some cases, the same thing can apply to the Knights as well.

Page of Wands

*Alternative Descriptions: The Princess of Wands, Knave or
Jack of Clubs, Rods, Batons or Staves*
*Esoteric Titles: Princess of the Shining Flame, Rose of the
Palace of Fire*

Character Type:

A young person of either sex with hazel or blue eyes and brown
hair. This card can also represent a person with a ruddy
complexion. As a personality type, he tends to be talkative (even
loud) and he is impossible to overlook or ignore.

Key Concepts:

This is the earthiest of the Fire cards, the basis or fuel for the flame, as it were. Therefore the Page or Princess represents the combustible material from which fire emerges.

Astrological Relationship:

Like the other Pages, this card is associated with one quadrant of the Earth from a point that is centered at the North Pole. This four-fold division takes in one quarter of the earth; thus the Page of Wands can symbolize Asia.

Correspondences:

In keeping with the fiery nature of the suit, leaping flames are included in the symbolism of the card, along with an altar and the color gold. A tiger's head is said to be the crest of the Page or Princess of Wands.

General Interpretation:

When viewed as a situation rather than as a person, the Page of Wands signifies messages and communications of all kinds. Urgent matters may demand your attention and others may press you for instant action, but you must take some time to consider your next move.

The Page can sometimes suggest a reunion with an old friend.

Positive Meaning:

This is a hard working, enthusiastic and adaptable person. He is anxious to please and to make a positive impression. The Page of Wands is charming and he has many interesting things to say—usually loudly. On the other hand, he may be hyperactive, prone to impatience and very impulsive. A firm direction is needed, because he finds distraction too easy. If this card applies to a calmer type of person, it suggests that boredom is unlikely, because the Page of Wands will always keep him on his toes. This Page may be a traveler or someone who brings you a surprising message.

Negative Meaning:

When the Page of Wands is reversed, this can reveal a rather spoiled and demanding individual. This is someone who moans and continually complains while stirring up trouble (an old nickname for the card is "the Gravedigger"). It may simply show that bad news is on its way, and in this case, the Page is simply the bearer of these ill tidings.

The card may also show educational difficulties or a problem with reading or writing.

Knight of Wands

Alternative Descriptions: Knight of Clubs, Rods, Batons or Staves
Esoteric Title: Prince of the Chariot of Fire

Character Type:

An energetic, vigorous young man with an athletic build and a healthy complexion. He often jumps to conclusions, he is impatient or he gives an impression of haste and having to be somewhere else.

Key Concepts:

This is the most fiery of the Fire cards. It symbolizes a wild blaze of great speed and intensity. Awesome in impact, the Knight of Wands is never forgotten.

Astrological Relationship:

Twenty-first degree of Scorpio to the twentieth degree of Sagittarius; approximately November 12 to December 10.

Correspondences:

The Knight of Wands' horse is black and he usually rides against a background of weaving flames. He bears a flaming torch and his cloak and heraldic mantling are scarlet while his crest is a winged, black horse's head.

General Interpretation:

This may foretell a move of house or premises. Another possibility is that a sudden, brilliant idea may propel you onto a new, exciting path. If the card is negative, then you could burn your bridges so that there is no going back.

Positive Meaning:

The Knight of Wands often represents a traveler or a visitor from afar. This Knight is a brave man; he has probably faced many trials and challenges and has overcome difficulties with the fortitude of a true and noble warrior. The person represented by this card is likely to be generous—often overly so.

He can be hasty when making judgments, so if he is not impressed in the first few seconds, then he is unlikely ever to change this swift opinion. Like a classical Sagittarian subject, the Knight of Wands is good-humored and he will prove to be a good friend and reliable ally.

Negative Meaning:

The impulsiveness of the reversed Knight is a problem. He can lose his temper very quickly, he is argumentative, combative and he may even be violent. His fiery nature forces him into conflict. He thrives on rivalry and feuds and may possess a bitter streak that grows out of jealousy or envy.

The word of this person, though given in good faith, will ultimately prove worthless.

Queen of Wands

*Alternative Descriptions: Queen of Clubs, Rods, Batons or
Staves*
*Esoteric Titles: Queen of the Thrones of Fire, Empress of
the Leaping Flames*

Character Type:

A dignified woman with a fiery and passionate temperament.
Her hair can be of any shade that is darker than blonde, often
inclining to red. Her coloring tends to be fair with hazel or blue
eyes.

Key Concepts:

The difficult concept of Water of Fire symbolizes a steady flame and a slow, steady course of action.

Astrological Relationship:

The twenty-first degree of Pisces to the twentieth degree of Aries; approximately March 11 to April 10.

Correspondences:

The leopard is the primary symbol associated with the Queen of Wands, although A.E. Waite makes this a cat in his version of the card. Her crest is a winged heraldic leopard or alternatively, a winged and flaming globe.

General Interpretation:

As an event card, the Queen of Wands warns against relying too heavily on the advice and actions of others.

Shyness may hamper communication and the advised course is to get out and about more.

Positive Meaning:

This is a passionate and intelligent lady. She is freedom loving, very lively and creatively gifted. It is quite likely that she is a businesswoman or that she is employed in an administrative position of some kind. Very practically minded, she has the gift of combining this admirable trait with a tender warm-heartedness. Thus she is an excellent organizer of both her own and other's affairs.

The Queen of Wands is popular, and her influence in business and social life is a good one. She helps those who are willing to help themselves. Traditionally, the Queen of Wands is said to prefer the countryside to the town and she is fascinated by the wonders of the natural world.

Negative Meaning:

The reversed Queen is likely to be mean, possessive and vengeful. Dictatorial by nature, she hates independence in others and she can bear a grudge for a long time. The hallmark of the reversed Queen of Wands is a bad temper and an envious spirit.

King of Wands

Alternative Descriptions: Prince of Wands. King of Clubs,
Rods, Batons or Staves
Esoteric Titles: Lord of the Flame, Lightning King of the
Spirits of Fire

King of Wands

Character Type:

A mature man with an air of authority. He is likely to be of athletic build. He is vigorous and he possesses a healthy constitution that is reflected in his complexion. His hair is probably brown and he has hazel or blue eyes.

Key Concepts:

The King is Air of Fire and therefore he represents a fierce blaze fanned by the intellectual wind. The card expresses the concept of increase, and therefore ambition, because as long as the wind keeps blowing, the fire reaches ever higher.

Astrological Relationship:

The twenty-first degree of Cancer to the twentieth degree of Leo; approximately July 12 to August 10.

Correspondences:

The Wand of this King should shed sparks and tongues of flame. He wears a crown of rays from which hangs a curtain of flame. The King's crest is the head of a lion, symbolic of the sign of Leo.

General Interpretation:

This card speaks of achieving psychological balance and gaining experience and wisdom. As a series of events, the card indicates a time when one's ideals and the practicalities of life merge, enabling you to act with integrity. If the card is reversed, then it is time to re-evaluate your motives.

Positive Meaning:

The King of Wands is likely to represent a man of the world, a professional person who is successful and who has traveled a great deal. He could easily be a businessman or at least employed in a managerial capacity. He is extremely honorable—even old-fashioned in the best possible sense. His word is his bond, he is a gentleman and he is just and proper. He is also very kind and he is noted for his generosity, although this latter trait may also be an excuse for him to show off.

As an advisor, the King of Wands is unbiased and wise. On a more intimate note, the fiery King of Wands is extremely passionate well into later life.

Negative Meaning:

The reversed King of Wands is likely to be a bigot, a person of very fixed opinions and he may have a belligerent manner. This is a man who wants his own way, and will think nothing of bullying others until he gets it.

Any advice that this King gives will be based solely on his own self-interest. This is a person whose own selfish desires and passions are paramount.

12

The Court Cards—The Suit of Coins

The King and Queen of Coins normally represent people in a reading. In this case, people with some kind of status. They may own land, have money or own enviable possessions. The Knight and Page can represent people or situations; in situations, these Coin cards talk of practical matters, resources, money and the need to deal with these things.

Note: Although the illustrations on your cards may show the Pages as male figures, or they may depict them as Princesses, and thus as female figures, these can refer to either sex. I have used the masculine "he" and "him" here to avoid clumsiness but do bear in mind that these cards are not gender specific. In some cases, the same thing can apply to the Knights as well.

The Page of Coins

Alternative Descriptions: The Knave, Jack, Child or
Princess of Pentacles, Disks or Spheres
Esoteric Titles: Princess of the Echoing Hills, Rose of the
Palace of Earth

Key Concepts:

This card is the earliest of the Coin Court cards. It is described as Earth of Earth. In Chinese philosophy, this would translate as "the Receptive," a perfect symbol for a young person starting out on the path of life.

Character Type:

A child or young person of either sex, usually with rich, brown hair and dark eyes.

Astrological Relationship:

In common with the other three Pages, the Page of Coins is considered to be associated with one quadrant of the Earth from a point on the North Pole. In this case, the Page is considered to indicate the continents of Europe and Africa.

Correspondences:

This Page is connected with the fruitfulness of the earth, which is said to include flowers, a wooded grove and lush grass. A ram's head and sheepskins may also be included in the symbolism.

General Interpretation:

The appearance of the Page of Coins can bring good news about money, travel in connection with business or a promotion at work. A youngster may soon do something that will make others proud of him, as long as the card is in the upright position.

Positive Meaning:

The Page of Coins represents a rather introverted young person with a mature head on his shoulders and a strong sense of duty. This Page is capable and conscientious, while force of circumstances makes him thrifty, so while he has little money at the moment, he has a lot going for him. With application, the Page of Coins will make an unmistakable mark on the world. The Page may represent a student or a person with considerable patience.

Negative Meaning:

An impatient and rather demanding young person who seems to have a constant need for money—usually someone else's. Someone who does not know the value of anything other than his own desires.

The Knight of Coins

Alternative Description: Knight of Pentacles, Disks or Spheres
Esoteric Title: Prince of the Chariot of Earth

Key Concepts:

The Knight of Coins represents Fire of Earth, and its image is a sluggishly flowing river of molten rock; also earthquakes and tectonic movements generally.

Character Type:

A young adult male, usually with dark hair and eyes.

Astrological Relationship:

Twenty-one degrees Leo to twenty degrees Virgo. These degrees cover roughly from August 14 to September 13. In northern climes this is harvest time, therefore this Knight is associated with the bountiful results of labor.

Correspondences:

A field of ripe corn, a light brown carthorse. This Knight's heraldic crest is said to be a winged stag's head.

General Interpretation:

Good news about all financial and business dealings. The restless nature of the Knight cards may show that business travel or rapid improvements in finances are in the offing.

Positive Meaning:

A practical and logical young man who does not like to take too many risks. This person may have to accept responsibility early in life, yet learns to cope with it well. He is a hard worker, so no challenge is too great for him, or task too daunting. This Knight is extremely trustworthy and will keep his word. Perhaps he might seem to be overly serious, but deep down he has an earthy and passionate nature.

Negative Meaning:

Do not be taken in by the reversed Knight's promises. He may have great ideas, but these will end up costing you money. This Knight is greedy and thinks only of himself. Perhaps plans for business travel should be put on hold.

The Queen of Coins

Alternative Description: Queen of Pentacles, Discs or
Spheres
Esoteric Titles: Queen of the Thrones of the Earth,
Empress of the Spirits of Earth

Key Concepts:

The Queen of Coins represents Water of Earth, thus the very force that nurtures and makes fruitful. The warm, fertile mud of a paddy field yielding many crops is a perfect image for this idea.

Character Type:

A mature woman, with dark hair and eyes. Possibly this queen is amply proportioned and generally cheerful.

Astrological Relationship:

The twenty-first degree of Sagittarius to the twentieth degree of Capricorn. This covers the period running up to Christmas, the New Year celebrations and the promise of a new chapter in life. The dates are from about December 13 to January 10.

Correspondences:

The goat symbol of the sign of Capricorn is connected to the card as both the Queen's crest and her companion. A golden orb is also suggestive of both rulership and completeness.

General Interpretation:

If the Queen does not represent a person, but a set of circumstances, it would denote over-anxiety in financial affairs. Perhaps money worries are getting the better of you.

Positive Meaning:

The Queen of Coins is known for her common sense, she is cheerful, hard to shock and has a good head for business. She is charitable and extremely kind hearted to those around her, but she does have a liking for luxury. Though occasionally prone to moods, she is basically very loving, in a maternal sort of way.

Negative Meaning:

When the Queen of Coins is reversed she becomes miserly and possessive. She is a stick in the mud and loathes change. She may be suspicious and mistrustful, placing more value on money than on anything else. Possibly lacking in morality, she will use every trick in the book in any dispute over cash. On the other hand, she may be a perfectly reasonable lady who is temporarily short of money.

The King of Coins

***Alternative Description: The Prince of Disks, King of
Pentacles, Disks or Spheres
Esoteric Titles: Lord of the Wild and Fertile Lands, King
of the Spirits of Earth***

King of Coins

Key Concepts:

This King represents the difficult concept of Air of Earth. This
seems to indicate high windy places, the tops of mountains, rocky
outcrops and the like, which provide a wide view over rolling
plains.

Character Type:

The King of Coins is usually a mature man of early middle age with dark hair and eyes. Possibly he is rather thick set in build. He may be connected with financial dealings or with agriculture.

Astrological Relationship:

Twenty-one degrees Aries to twenty degrees Taurus. The approximate dates governed by the King of Coins are April 11 to May 11. This period is just after the beginning of the astrological year, when spring planting is done. The King therefore expresses the concept of "As one sows so shall he reap."

Correspondences:

The head of an ox or bull, signifying the sign of Taurus, and the responsibility of protection that a bull has to the members of his herd. The King of Coins, like the queen, possesses a golden orb symbolizing his earthly power. The cross above the orb shows the four cardinal directions.

General Interpretation:

The card advises resolute and decisive action and urges one to discard any doubts about one's own abilities. When upright, this is a card of good fortune in all matters connected with finances and property. If reversed, then the King of Coins may warn against unfair or underhand financial dealings.

Positive Meaning:

This King is a shrewd realist. He is practical and reasonable, an ideal businessman. He could be a bank manager, farmer or someone of considerable wealth. Even so, he tends to be rather unpretentious with a calm, stable personality, and is slow to anger. The King of Coins tends to be married and fond of his family, or at least in a pretty settled mode of life. He is a tough but honest man in all his dealings.

Negative Meaning:

An unimaginative, mean and fairly stupid individual who is basically corrupt. He may associate with gamblers and dishonest elements. He is greedy and possessive and does not wish the questioner any good at all.

13

The Court Cards—The Suit of Swords

The King and Queen of Swords normally represent people in a reading. In this case, people with some kind of status. They may own land, have money or own enviable possessions. The Knight and Page can represent people or situations; in situations, they may indicate legal or medical matters and sometimes aggression, assertion or the need to know what is going on. These cards suggest that a situation has arisen that cannot be shelved.

Note: Although the illustrations on your cards may show the Pages as male figures, or they may depict them as Princesses, and thus as female figures, these can refer to either sex. I have used the masculine "he" and "him" here to avoid clumsiness, but do bear in mind that these cards are not gender specific. In some cases, the same thing can apply to the Knights as well.

Page of Swords

Alternative Description: The Princess, Knave or Jack of Swords
Esoteric Titles: Princess of the Rushing Winds, Lotus of the Palace of Air

Key Concepts:

This is the most earthy of the Swords court cards and can be described as Earth of Air. Therefore, there is intelligence, but it is weighed down and suffocated by anxieties. In Chinese philosophy this combination means "troubles."

Character Type:

A young person with dark hair, pale skin, sharply defined features and penetrating eyes.

Astrological Relationship:

The Page of Swords is associated with the westerly quadrant of the globe from a point that is centered on the North Pole. It is therefore symbolically connected to the two American continents.

Subsidiary Symbols:

Among the correspondences for the Page of Swords are listed a silver altar, cirrus clouds, drawn blades and rising smoke. The Page's crest is the head of the gorgon Medusa.

General Interpretation:

If this card does not represent a person, then you are being instructed to be as cool as you can. The card warns of hidden dangers. You may be the victim of malice and slander. Legal disputes may be indicated.

Positive Meaning:

The Page of Swords has a perceptive intelligence and an extremely swift wit. Thus, it is difficult to deceive this Page, and it may indeed be unwise to attempt to do so. This is because the Page of Swords has the reputation for being vengeful. However, the Page has a knack of turning apparent misfortunes to advantage. As with most of the Swords Court cards, the Page is scheming and eloquent and he can use this latter ability as a weapon. His words can be cutting. On the other hand, the Page of Swords possesses immense curiosity and he is anxious to learn. This Page may bring you into contact with helpful people, provide good news and he may act as a spy on your behalf. He will prove to be an ingenious ally.

Negative Meaning:

All the traits of the positive Page are used against you when the card is reversed. This is a slanderer, a clever liar and a malicious seeker of vengeance who wishes you ill. He or she may be bitter over a past hurt or an imagined wrong. This person is very secretive yet very clever and he may attempt to worm his way into your confidence for dark reasons of his own.

Knight of Swords

Esoteric Title: Prince of the Chariot of Air

Knight of Swords

Key Concepts:

The Knight of Swords is Fire of Air and is expressive of the violent motion of tempests, hurricanes and sudden storms. He is particularly associated with lightning, striking swiftly and then moving on.

Character Type:

A tall, dark man with charm, wit and insight. He may be eccentric and he rarely has any patience with convention.

Astrological Relationship:

Twenty-first degree of Taurus to the twentieth degree of Gemini; approximately May 10 to June 9.

Subsidiary Symbols:

The Knight of Swords rides a brown horse that has wings in a similar fashion to the mythical Pegasus. Drawn blades and wild, windswept clouds are other symbols. His crest is a hexagram or six-pointed star with attached wings.

General Interpretation:

A whirlwind of events is about to confuse all the issues in your life. Circumstances will suddenly and inexplicably change and other people will react in unpredictable ways. If the card is reversed, then prepare yourself for a fight.

Positive Meaning:

The Knight of Swords is extremely courageous, tough and intelligent. He possesses the gift of eloquence and is therefore attractive and charming. He has been likened to a sudden storm, blowing into your life with no warning, occasionally causing havoc and then blowing out again just as swiftly as he arrived. Being so intelligent, the Knight requires a lot of mental stimulation to keep his interest. His great fault is that he becomes bored very quickly. The same cannot be said of the lives of those who come into contact with him. His impetuosity ensures that any dealings one has with this bold Knight and his adventures are fascinating, as are the often highly colored tales he relates about his exploits!

Negative Meaning:

The reversed Knight of Swords has very little staying power and he is a magnet to trouble. He may display a violent streak and he is secretive, possibly treacherous, very plausible and always ready with an excuse for his behavior. He is a clever liar, and he is very rarely caught.

Queen of Swords

Esoteric Titles: Queen of the Thrones of Air, Empress of the Clouds

Key Concepts:

The Queen of Swords is Water of Air and therefore expresses rain. Emotion and intellect are united in this card.

Character Type:

A tall, slightly built woman with pale skin, thin lips and dark hair. Her eyes may be dark or shades of gray, blue or green. She has a maturity of attitude and she is a mistress of disapproving looks.

Tradition states that she very independent, probably a widow or divorcee.

Astrological Relationship:

The twenty-first degree of Virgo to the twentieth degree of Libra; approximately September 10 to October 10.

Subsidiary Symbols:

The symbols associated with the Swords Queen are the severed head of a man and cumulus clouds. Her heraldic crest is the winged head of a child.

General Interpretation:

Focus on your goals, because concentration on an objective will overcome all obstacles. If reversed, the card shows insincerity, scheming and interference. If the card refers to you, then you may be too clever and too manipulative for your own good.

Positive Meaning:

The Queen of Swords represents an extremely independent person. Her logical mind is capable of high intelligence and she tends to approach every problem with cool calculation. This Queen is noted for her physical grace and she may be fond of music and dancing. She is intellectually acute and she hates to waste time, so her spare moments are usually taken up with reading. Very little will get past her keen perception. She is extremely alert to the undercurrents in the lives of those around her, so it would be a mistake to underestimate either her logic or her intuition.

Negative Meaning:

In some cases, the reversed Queen of Swords is a prude—or at least one who lives by a set of old-fashioned established rules that are extremely strict and inflexible. She may be bitter as a result of past hurts and she is a harsh critic of other people's morals. It would be wise to remember that the reversed Queen of Swords is capable of extreme jealousy. She can therefore be malicious and quite dangerous. If she acts as a go-between, she is likely to stir up trouble by telling half-truths and outright falsehoods.

King of Swords

Alternative Description: The Prince of Swords
Esoteric Titles: Lord of the Winds and Breezes, King of the
Spirits of Air

Key Concepts:

This is the most intellectual and lofty of the Swords, being Air of Air.

Character Type:

A tall, dark man with dark-brown, piercing eyes. The card is mainly concerned with this person's intelligence and critical faculties, so the physical characteristics described here are less important.

Astrological Relationship:
The twenty-first degree of Capricorn to the twentieth degree of Aquarius; approximately January 10 to February 9.

Subsidiary Symbols:
Winged sylphs or elemental spirits of the air are symbolic of this king, as indeed are all clouds. The crest of the King of Swords is the head of an angel.

General Interpretation:
You need to take charge of events and to use your willpower to gain control of your own life, and possibly to make decisions for others as well. If the card is reversed, the opposite is the case and you may find yourself being controlled, powerless and manipulated.

Positive Meaning:
Traditional card reading suggests that the King of Swords is a judge, lawyer, doctor or other highly qualified professional person. Indeed it is quite likely that this card represents an authority figure. He is someone in a position of trust and responsibility. In terms of personality, he will be cool and calm, disliking overt displays of emotion that would disturb his mental equilibrium. Logical and reasonable, the King is happiest in the mental realms of rationality. His very intelligence creates boredom, and this prompts him to seek out less organized souls, simply because he needs the mental stimulation they can provide.

Negative Meaning:
The negative interpretation of this card is similar to the upright version, although in this case the reversed King is more mistrustful and he is a very harsh critic and judge. His mental powers are very

acute, although he tends not to analyze his own views and actions. He may be a bigot, prone to unfounded suspicions and manipulative mind-games. He is likely to be deceitful and he could symbolize a schemer or confidence trickster.

14

The Court Cards—The Suit of Cups

The King and Queen of Cups normally represent people in a reading. In this case, people who are loving, kind and friendly and who may be able to give sympathetic advice. The Knight and Page can represent people or situations; in situations, they may mark the start of a love relationship or a pleasant friendship. Sometimes these people or situations are not as satisfactory as one would wish them to be.

Note: Although the illustrations on your cards may show the Pages as male figures, or they may depict them as Princesses, and thus as female figures, these can refer to either sex. I have used the masculine "he" and "him" here to avoid clumsiness, but do bear in mind that these cards are not gender specific. In some cases, the same thing can apply to the Knights as well.

Page of Cups

Alternative Description: The Princess, Knave or Jack of Cups
Esoteric Titles: Princess of the Waters, Lotus of the Palace of the Floods

Page of Cups

Key Concepts:

This is the earthiest of the Cup Court cards. It is described as Earth of Water and represents the power of the emotions to create substance, ideas and form. Earth represents matter in its solid state, therefore Earth of Water can be thought of as frozen water or ice.

Character Type:

A child or young person of either sex, usually with fair hair, pale skin and dreamy blue eyes. The affectionate Cups Page usually possesses a soft voice and he is often insecure and in need of emotional security and approval.

Astrological Relationship:

In common with the Pages of the other suits, the Page of Cups is symbolically associated with a quadrant of the Earth that is centered upon a point in the North Pole. Aptly enough, since this is a watery suit, the area of the globe the card symbolizes is the largest expanse of water on the planet, which is the Pacific Ocean.

Subsidiary Symbols:

The crest of this Page is the graceful swan. Golden Dawn sources also state that a turtle should emerge from the cup, although in the Waite pack the turtle is replaced by a fish. Sea spray, a lotus and a dolphin provide subsidiary symbols.

General Interpretation:

When the Page of Cups represents a series of events rather than a person, then falling head over heels in love would be a reasonable interpretation. However it may not be such a good idea to surrender one's heart, because practical matters such as the need to study for exams may also need to be addressed.

Positive Meaning:

The Page of Cups is gentle, sensitive and deeply emotional. Creative gifts are indicated as well as an insightful and intuitive nature. If the Page describes a girl, then she will tend to be tomboyish, if a boy then slightly feminine. Either way, this is a young person who needs reassurance and guidance. It is important to bear in mind that this card does not always indicate a young person. The Page of Cups can be any age, but is always young at heart.

Negative Meaning:

When reversed, the card can show someone who is spoiled and who has shallow, trivial attitudes. This is someone who plays upon the sympathies of others, and he can be very petulant when thwarted. It may also indicate someone who lives in a dream world, and he is likely to become very angry when reality does not live up to the fantasy that he has created.

Knight of Cups

Esoteric Title: Prince of the Chariot of Water

Key Concepts:

The Knight of Cups represents the difficult concept of Fire of Water. This can be thought of as a swift, passionate downpour of rain or as rushing, bubbling streams and springs.

Character Type:

A young adult male, usually with fair hair, pale skin and blue eyes. He is often casually dressed and possesses a worldly, yet bohemian air. Often well traveled, he is very aware of fashion and cultural developments around the world.

Astrological Relationship:

The twenty-first degree of Aquarius to the twentieth degree of Pisces; approximately February 10 to March 9.

Subsidiary Symbols:

The Knight of Cups' horse is white, and a crab symbolic of the sign of Cancer emerges from his cup. The Knight's crest is a peacock with open wings and tail.

General Interpretation:

If the Knight card does not relate to a person, then it is likely that sudden changes to your emotional state are to be expected. Love affairs beginning with an instant attraction are likely. If the card is reversed, then your feelings may be abused.

Positive Meaning:

The primary meaning of the Knight of Cups is the arrival of a new lover or a good friend. As a character, this Knight is enthusiastic, passionate and amiable. He may be poetic and gifted artistically. He is certainly charming and attractive and he can empathize with the feelings of others. This person is an ally in the emotional sense. This card often indicates good news, and it can indicate that opportunities and offers of an emotional nature are on their way. It may also show that beneficial changes are about to occur within your close relationships.

Negative Meaning:

When the Knight of Cups is reversed, a lover will soon depart. However this is a blessing in disguise because the character of this

Knight is not pleasant, even though he may be very good looking. The reversed Knight reveals an immoral nature, fickle attentions and faithlessness.

Queen of Cups

Esoteric Titles: Queen of the Thrones of the Waters,
Empress of the Rivers and Fountains

Queen of Cups

Key Concepts:

The Queen of Cups is Water of Water and is therefore emotion
doubled. This concept is one of receptivity and reflection.

Character Type:

A pale-featured lady with fair hair. This Queen can also represent a woman who is beautiful with fine features. Her eyes are expressive and her physical sensuality is evident in her movements.

Astrological Relationship:

The twenty-first degree of Gemini to the twentieth degree of Cancer; approximately June 10 to July 10.

Subsidiary Symbols:

The symbols of the Queen of Cups are reminiscent of those appearing in the Moon card in the Major Arcana. Another symbol is a crayfish or a lobster emerging from a river, as depicted on the Moon card, which is associated with the sign of Pisces. This builds a connection between the Queen of Cups and the sign of Pisces. The Queen's crest is an Ibis.

General Interpretation:

Issues of the heart predominate when this card does not represent a person. A declaration of love is indicated, as is a flowering of creative potential. A reversed Queen of Cups may show a lack of logic.

Positive Meaning:

The Queen of Cups is very imaginative and she tends to be artistically gifted. She is poetic, dreamy and deeply sympathetic. She is also sociable, but she is likely to lose confidence if she is in the company of those who are too critical or dominant, so she must choose her companions carefully. The Queen of Cups often loves dancing, music and romance itself. She is honest, loyal and caring, with a sweet disposition and a charitable nature. This is a woman who follows the dictates of her heart and tries to create harmony and happiness around her. She is also empathetic and in tune with the emotions of her companions.

Negative Meaning:

The reversed Queen of Cups is likely to be immoral and vain. She can be deceitful and extremely perverse, constantly demanding that others indulge her idle whims. Her own petty desires are the only things that are important to her, and she may control others by a display of weakness that forces them to pander to her. She is a drain on the emotional and financial resources of others. Alternatively, the reversed Queen may indicate a false lover.

King of Cups

Alternative Description: Prince of Cups
Esoteric Titles: Lord of the Waves and Waters, King of the
Hosts of the Sea

King of Cups

Key Concepts:

This King is described as Air of Water and this is thought to be volatile, expressing the release of pent up energy such as steam. Clouds too can be thought of as Air of Water.

Character Type:

A charming mature man with considerable sophistication. He usually has fair or gray hair and pale blue eyes. He has achieved much in life.

Astrological Relationship:

The twenty-first degree of Libra to the twentieth degree of Scorpio; approximately October 10 to November 10.

Subsidiary Symbols:

The symbols of the King of Cups are those of the sign of Scorpio. These include an eagle-serpent issuing from a lake, or a scorpion. His crest is an imperial eagle.

General Interpretation:

When the King of Cups does not represent a person, then you will soon find yourself mediating between two factions. You will need charm and diplomacy to defuse a difficult situation. When the card is reversed, then resolution of conflict is impossible.

Positive Meaning:

The King of Cups is charismatic. He may not be conventionally good looking, but is nonetheless attractive. He shows affection and he receives love in return. Very loyal, he is warm-hearted, kindly and responsible. Extremely sociable, this King is at the heart of any gathering. He is possessed of a deep reservoir of inner strength. It is likely that he has gained this resilience the hard way, because he has been through emotionally testing times in the past. The King of Cups enjoys comfort and may be creative. If not, then he will be very appreciative of the arts.

Negative Meaning:

The card in the reversed position reveals a rather sad figure who is adept at covering up his weaknesses. This person is usually very secretive because of his vulnerability. He may possess a bad temper and he can inflict his own emotional pain on others. He may also have an addictive personality, and he may be prone to secret vices. This card sometimes indicates a dependence on alcohol, drugs or gambling.

15

The Major Arcana

We have already looked at the possible origins of the Major Arcana of the Tarot and its relationship to both astrology and the Qabalah, but now we will look at each card in turn. In the succeeding chapters, you will find the Qabalistic, astrological and symbolic associations for each card. In addition, you will find descriptions of some of the important symbolism that is shown in a modern Tarot deck. In those cases where the illustrations differed from the ones that are familiar to us now, I mention these illustrations of the past, along with their symbolism. Then I outline the symbolism that is encapsulated in each card, followed by interpretations for both upright and reversed cards.

The interpretations in this book are as close to the early ideas as possible, but without harking so far back into history as to make their meanings difficult for a modern card reader to interpret or to explain to his inquirer. For instance, there would hardly be any point in talking about the actions of a King or his courtiers in countries where such people do not exist—or if they do exist, where they no longer have the power to influence the lives of ordinary people. The interpretations in this book may be somewhat different from those that any modern day Tarot reader wishes to use, but that is the whole point of this book. We all know that Tarot is an interpretive art, and that a successful reader will always put his own spin on any card or on any combination of cards that appear in a reading. I do not for one moment wish to say that the interpretations in this book are "right," and that any other interpretation must be "wrong." My only desire is to give you interpretations that are as close as possible to their older symbolic meanings. Naturally, you must always feel free to use your own deck of cards in your own inimitable way.

I know that modern Tarot readers rarely use reversed cards. As it happens, I only read a reversed card myself when one gets turned around by accident. Tarot specialists of bygone days did use reversed cards, which is why they must be included in this book.

Here is a tip that does not reach back to the past. The ratio of cards in a deck is roughly one-third Major Arcana to two thirds Minor Arcana cards. If a spread shows a disproportionate number of Major Arcana cards, then the events surrounding the inquirer are in the hands of fate and they may be quite considerable. If the cards are balanced, there seems to be a balance between the forces of karma and destiny on one side and the inquirer's ability to direct his life on the other. Even when there are few Major Arcana cards in evidence, the inquirer's life can be eventful, but things are more likely to be in his hands than in the hands of fate. However, in this case a lone Major Arcana card can assume an outstanding role within the reading. The message here is always to watch those Major cards, as they are an extremely powerful indicator of the shape of things to come.

Unnumbered, or 0

The Fool

Alternative Titles: The Joker, The Madman
Esoteric Title: Spirit of Ether

Qabalistic Letter: Aleph, meaning ox. Number value 1.

Tree of Life Pathway: First, between Kether and Chockmah.

Direction: Above to Below.

Astrological Correspondence:
Originally the Fool was assigned to the element of Air, but in recent years it has become customary to allocate the unpredictable influence of the planet Uranus to this card.

Description:
The basic image on this card is that of a jester who is dressed in "motley" with a cap and bells. In old Tarot decks, the Fool is often bearded, but in more modern designs his youthfulness is emphasized. Many versions of the card also feature a small dog, or very occasionally a cat. This animal either accompanies the Fool on his wanderings or attacks him. Sometimes, the Fool's trousers or hose are shown falling down, revealing his bare behind. Cards dating from the nineteenth century onwards often show the Fool walking towards a cliff edge with his eyes elevated so that he does not see the abyss that is before him. Some designs fix his gaze on a butterfly that flutters just out of reach. One feature that tends to remain in the card is the stick that the Fool holds over his shoulder and the knotted handkerchief or sack that hangs from it.

Symbolism:
This is the wide-eyed eternal traveler who is ready for anything, and who, his mind open and free, is setting off for the unknown adventure. Some would call him mad, most would consider that he is not ready for the journey that lies before him, but ready or not—here he comes!

The character of the Fool is that of the holy innocent. He is trusting, a stranger to falsehood and cynicism. He is a breath of fresh air, loving life and the adventure that beckons him. He is ready for opportunity; he is open for it because he has no preconceptions. Equally, the Fool has no fear of what awaits him. Even the cliff edge holds no terror for him. After all, the Fool is light on his feet and nimble enough to deal with that peril when it arises, despite the warnings of his faithful dog, which sees the danger that is ahead of him. No, the Fool's eyes are fixed on his dreams, which are symbolized by the butterfly, and only the greatest cynic would say that he is wrong (the word "cynic" derives from the Greek for dog). In short, the Fool is ready to "take the plunge!"

The freedom of the Fool is associated with the element of Air. He is like the breeze, at home nowhere and everywhere, and traveling from place to place with no responsibility except to himself. In recent times the Fool has become associated with the planet Uranus (a word derived from the Greek for sky). Astrologically, this planet expresses the ability to receive sudden inspiration, to break free of bonds and to overcome obsolete notions. It also promotes eccentricity and can lead one to court dangerous situations.

The card's Hebrew letter is Aleph, which means "ox," and this has more than one symbolic connotation. Firstly the ox implies wealth; ancient economies were often based on cattle. Secondly, it implies the notion of sacrifice, due to the choicest ox being given to the divine power. Abraham was commanded to sacrifice his beloved son Isaac on Mount Moriah, Jesus was sacrificed at Golgotha, while, in a less physical sense, the Buddha sacrificed his earthly attachment.

Aleph has no sound in Hebrew. Instead it is either an inhalation or an exhalation of breath. It is both a gasp of wonder and a preparation to make a noise or to speak, sing or shout. In concept, it is related to Chi or Prana, the cosmic life-breath, the life force, the vital energetic animating principle, the very essence of creativity in the universe. the Fool is the zero, the nothing from which all creation proceeds.

Upright Meaning:

This is simultaneously the first and the last card of the Tarot sequence and a link between the two. As the first card, it acts as a preliminary to that which will follow and has strong associations with childhood, innocence and new beginnings. As the last card, it is a sigh of relief and an indicator of a new and exciting departure.

It is said that "fools rush in where angels fear to tread," because the sense of wide-eyed wonder is combined with a bravery that has its roots in simple naiveté. Yet it is this very carelessness that provides the protection. the Fool's head may be in the clouds with pitfalls and perils all around him, yet he is completely safe. His innocence and optimism are his guardians, as indeed they will be yours.

Anything can happen when this card appears. There will be a new road to travel to who knows where, but the prospect of the journey will be exciting and the potential for fun along the way is endless. Every mishap and danger will be worth putting up with, for the wonders you will see on your journey will ensure that you would not miss it for anything in the world. One thing is certain, you are going to learn a lot along the way and eventually you will turn that original innocence into life experience.

Medieval Italian tradition suggests that if the Fool appears as the first card in a reading, the question asked is probably the wrong one, or that you are not ready to ask it. It may be that your initial assumptions are mistaken or that you want to know the answer for the wrong reasons.

Reversed Meaning:

When the card is upright it is a good idea to forge ahead, to leap before you look, but when the Fool is reversed, the opposite is the case, and great caution should be exercised. The reversed Fool warns against impulsive decisions and foolish whims that can lead you into danger. You may be acting in an irrational or immature manner. A brutally realistic look at your life is called for, otherwise you could literally become—and be seen as—the fool.

I (1)

The Magician

Alternative Titles: The Juggler, The Minstrel, The Magus
Esoteric Title: Magus of Power

Qabalistic Letter: Beth, meaning house. Number value 2.

Tree of Life Pathway: Second, between Kether and Binah.

Direction: Above.

Astrological Correspondence:
The Magician is aptly assigned to the planet Mercury.

Description:
This card originally showed a sly, smiling fairground huckster standing at a table with various items, such as a kettle, knives, dice and cups laying on it. In his right hand he holds a magic wand, in his left a coin or ball. In some old versions he appears to be performing the "cup and ball" trick, a profitable if unscrupulous illusion that is as popular now as it ever was. On his head, this devious juggler wears a large, floppy brimmed hat. In more modern versions of the card the Magician takes on a far more dignified, spiritual aspect. No longer is his table covered in the paraphernalia of cheap conjuring, but with the four suit emblems of the Minor Arcana. His robes are red and white, his belt is a serpent eating its own tail and above his head, a lemniscate appears. This is the symbol of eternity that resembles a figure eight on its side. In short, the Magician is no longer a glib confidence trickster, but a figure who exudes occult power. The furthest symbolic distance from the original "showman" card is found in the Tarot of Aleister Crowley, in which the Magician is shown as the god Mercury, complete with winged heels.

Symbolism:
The Hebrew letter associated with the Magician is Beth. This letter has two sounds; "B" and "V." In Tarot terms, the double-letters are associated with the seven planets known to antiquity, so the Magician is astrologically associated with the planet Mercury.

The first letter in the Hebrew Bible is Beth, starting the word borayshice or vereysheet, depending upon which form of Hebrew pronunciation one uses. This means "In the beginning." By the same token, the Greek word Genesis was originally borayshice in Hebrew. Thus card 1 is the start, although it doesn't appear to be so, coming as it does after the silent letter, Aleph. Aleph stands for the Fool, the pause (before taking action), the intake of breath, and the link between the end and the beginning. So confusion arises because Beth equates to 2. the Fool is all and everything, a singularity; but the Magician says, "this is what I am, everything else is something else." It is the first expression of individuality. This is an interesting point, since, astrologically, Mercury is associated with early childhood, with verbal self-expression and the ability to use the mind to ask questions.

The literal meaning of Beth is "house" or a home for energy, so the potential of everything is found in this letter. It can also refer to the physical body or the individual mind, the "house" of the soul.

One of the earliest books of the Qabalah states that "Beth reigns in wisdom." If the Egyptian origin of the Tarot is considered, the concept of the god Thoth must be brought into play. Thoth, the "ever-wise," evolved into Hermes Trismagestus or Hermes the Thrice Great. He was the supposed inventor of mathematics and writing, and thought to be the architect of the pyramids and the inventor of more arcane arts such as numerology, alchemy and astrology. One of Hermes/Thoth's most influential statements is a very brief explanation of astrology: "As above, so below." With this in mind, it is interesting to note that the Tarot Magician's right hand points upward while his left is inclined in a downward direction. Hermes is the Greek version of the Roman god, Mercury.

The four suits of the Minor Arcana that are displayed on the table in most modern variants of the card are said to represent the four precepts of witchcraft and magic (as well as the four elements); to know, to dare, to will and to keep silent. The upraised wand in the Magician's right hand is the symbol of a herald or messenger, but it also recalls the Caduceus or staff of Mercury, which could be used to induce sleep or to ward off slumber, thus illustrating that the use of power has two sides.

Upright Meaning:

In Tarot interpretation, this card is number one, showing the start of a new enterprise that requires initiative, willpower and a vision of the future. The Magician indicates a sense of purpose, dynamism and the ability to cope with new circumstances. There is usually an element of uncertainty about the card, because a new beginning is often beset by unforeseen difficulties and teething troubles. Yet the Magician promises that with a little ingenuity you will succeed in whatever you set out to do.

The ability to think on your feet, with perhaps wit and the odd bluff or two (we mustn't forget the Magician's mercurial nature), will get you past any difficulties. Ironic humor is also a factor here; you are bound to have a chuckle when you have succeeded.

The Magician is a particularly good card to see if you are considering a major departure in your life. The card shows that there is plenty of potential and it is up to you to deploy shrewdness so as to get your plans off the ground. If you are faced with opposition, the appearance of the Magician shows that your own cunning and wiles will ensure that you are several steps ahead of those who would hold you back. The card reveals that you could out-think, out-talk and out-pace any rivals.

Apart from its more general interpretation, this card often represents a man, the questioner himself if male or the special man in a woman's life. However, she needs to be warned that this man can be the worthy suitor that he appears to be, or conversely, someone with an eye on the main chance.

Reversed Meaning:

The reversed Magician can indicate a confidence trickster or an extremely plausible liar. If an opportunity is presented to you, then be very suspicious of the other's motives. New enterprises are likely to fail or they may be designed to part you from your cash.

II (2)

The High Priestess

*Alternative Titles: The Papess, The Female Pope, Pope
Joan, The Priestess, Juno
Esoteric Title: Priestess of the Silver Star*

Qabalistic Letter: Gimel, meaning camel. Number value 3.

Tree of Life Pathway: Third, from Kether to Tiphareth.

Direction: Below.

Astrological Correspondence:
    The High Priestess is a planetary card symbolically connected to the Moon.

Description:
    Traditionally, this mysterious card was called the Female Pope, Pope Joan or the Papess. It showed a robed lady dressed somewhat like a nun, enthroned between two pillars. Between the pillars hangs a veil or curtain. On her head she bears the triple tiara usually worn at papal coronations. In her lap she holds an open book. More modern versions of this card add lunar symbolism, such as replacing the papal tiara with a crown showing the phases of the moon. The Book is also sometimes replaced with a scroll often marked "Torah" which is the Jewish bible. The two pillars behind the High Priestess' throne are usually colored black and white, and they are sometimes marked with a J and a B. These stand for Jakin and Boaz, the names of the Qabalistic pillars of severity and mercy (also the names of two sons of wise King Solomon). In some Tarot decks, the High Priestess card is dispensed with entirely and replaced with a figure of the goddess Juno, the wife of Jupiter, who is shown with her emblem, which is the peacock.

Symbolism:
    Although much is made of the lunar connections to the High Priestess, there is little doubt that its image is based on a well-known medieval legend. The tale, which was first committed to writing in the thirteenth century by a Dominican monk, Stephen of Bourbon, tells of some strange events, which are said to have occurred five hundred years earlier. These apocryphal events

concerned an exceptionally educated young Englishwoman named Joan who eloped with a handsome Benedictine monk. The guilty couple fled to Athens, whereupon Joan adopted male clerical attire as a disguise and she took the name of Johannes Angelicus, or John of England. However, Joan's Benedictine lover suddenly died, so she made her way to Rome—still disguised as a man, presumably for her safety. Such was Joan's piety that she quickly rose through the ranks of the church hierarchy and eventually became a cardinal. In 855 A.D. Pope Leo IV died, and the pious Cardinal Johannes was elected his successor. However, Pope Joan was not destined to enjoy a long reign because during the procession through the city following the papal coronation, Her Holiness was overcome by labor pains (either on the steps of St. Peter's or outside the Coliseum) and promptly gave birth to a child. Pope Joan expired on the spot sparking off riots that engulfed Rome and placed the church itself in peril. It is said that every subsequent Pope has been physically examined to ensure that such a scandal could not occur again.

So much for anti-clerical legend, but as far as the card is concerned, modern commentators have associated the High Priestess with the moon or at least with one of the three aspects of the lunar orb, which is the maiden. The other two aspects are the mother and the hag, and these are likely to be represented by the Empress and the Moon cards. The Priestess's crown tends to be triple in nature, and it is either a papal coronet, as in older versions of the card, or the moon in its three phases as in the more contemporary versions.

The veil behind her is symbolic both of mystery and of virginity. The two pillars, black and white, are the outer verticals of the Tree of Life, the pillar of severity and the pillar of mercy. While still on Qabalistic matters, the Hebrew letter associated with the Priestess is Gimel, meaning camel. A camel is the "ship of the desert" connecting distant places across an arid wilderness. Likewise, the pathway of the Priestess is the longest on the Tree of Life, crossing the abyss from Tiphareth to Kether.

Upright Meaning:

In a woman's reading, this card may represent the lady herself, while in a man's reading, the High Priestess often represents the woman in his life. The card can also symbolize inspiration, especially the kind that is associated with the muse.

The High Priestess indicates that whatever your question happens to be, you do not yet have all the facts, even if you think that you do! The card often represents a wise guide who will help you. This guide may be an actual person, usually a woman, though it may represent the faculties of intuition, memory, instinct and psychic ability that will serve to chart your path.

The card is considered to be scholarly, so it is a good omen for studies and the deepening of knowledge. The veil that hangs behind the Priestess hints at a secret that you suspect exists but whose nature is concealed from you for the time being. The truth will soon come out and you will need a touch of inspiration and intuitive wisdom to put the new information to good use. In a case such as this, your own instincts and your gut feeling will be your best guide. There is a hint that these inner feelings may derive from some higher power.

Reversed Meaning:

Careless remarks can be wounding when the card is reversed. Secrets may be unwisely revealed and passions may overrule common sense. Sexual tensions and frustrations can be a problem, too. This can also indicate that you are spending too much time looking after other people's welfare at the expense of your own. Should you feel that the card represents a particular person, then this is one whose morals are distinctly lacking or one who has a moody and hysterical nature.

III (3)

The Empress

*Alternative Title: During the French Revolution, all hints
of royalty were edited from the cards, so this card was
shown with the crown and shield removed and the
Empress was re-titled The Grandmother.
Esoteric Title: Daughter of the Mighty Ones*

Qabalistic Letter: Daleth, meaning door. Number value 4.

Tree of Life Pathway: Fourth, between Binah and Chockmah.

Direction: East.

Astrological Correspondence:
The Empress is a planetary trump associated with Venus.

Description:
Like the previous card, the High Priestess, the Empress sits crowned and enthroned, often holding a shield and a scepter. In some old Tarot designs she also appears to be winged, but this may just be a badly drawn attempt to depict the back of her throne. Many versions of the card show an imperial eagle on her shield, probably to emphasize that this is an Empress, rather than a Queen, of the Minor Arcana. Other decks emblazon the shield with the astrological symbol of the planet Venus. The Imperial crown is often adorned with twelve small stars, while her scepter may be mistaken for a hand mirror or another depiction of the Venus symbol. More modern decks show the Empress seated in lush countryside. Some show her to be pregnant or suckling an infant. Occasionally the Empress is depicted with a cornucopia or horn of plenty.

Symbolism:
Just as an Emperor is a king of kings and the father of his empire, so the Empress is the great queen and the mother of her equally important domain. The French Revolutionary title of the card "The Grandmother" is strangely apt in this regard, because the image of the Empress is a depiction of the pagan Great Mother. Here it is identified with the warm and passionate goddess Venus, just as her more virginal lunar aspect is found in the High Priestess card.

Venus is the amorous Roman version of the primordial goddess. By the time of Julius Caesar (who claimed this deity as his ancestor), Venus had become the goddess of love, but originally she was far more than the fickle arbiter of amour. Once she had been acclaimed as "Venus Genatrix," the wave-born mother of all. She is Mother Nature personified, eternally pregnant, generating life, giving the bounty of creation and reigning over the rhythm of the world.

The Empress is the doorway to new life, and the Hebrew letter associated with the card is Daleth, literally meaning "door." Daleth is a double letter with two sounds, which in Tarot terms makes it planetary in nature; in this case, of course, it is symbolically connected to Venus, the morning star.

In the Qabalistic Cube, the Empress holds the East, the door of the dawning sun. The Empress' door has also been compared to the womb as the gateway of life. The door is also a barrier necessary for privacy, security, storage, conservation and comfort. It may be regarded as the door (Daleth) to the house (Beth) of the Magician. It may also be thought of as the doorway in which the Hanged Man is suspended. In this case, the Hanged Man may be considered to symbolize the trials of birth. There is another connection with the twelfth card, because the Empress is often shown with twelve stars in her crown representing the signs of the zodiac. Indeed she has been described as "the star-crowned Empress, herself the morning star."

Upright Meaning:

The fertile Empress signals a time of prosperity and joy. The card indicates material comfort and hints at someone with whom to share contentment. The Empress card is symbolically associated with the springtime and is therefore also associated with the fruitfulness of the earth and the fertility of both human beings and animals. It is not surprising, then, that the appearance of the Empress is often an indicator of pregnancy. In essence, the card is maternal in nature and can show emotional support, protectiveness and a resultant feeling of security. This is a card of reassurance and love. Its appearance in a reading will show that everything will turn out all right in the end, and that even if you get a few bruises and scrapes along the way, you will have someone to kiss it better and hug you while telling you how well you have done.

The Empress can sometimes indicate moving to a new home. This is especially true if you enjoy decorating or gardening and if you also love to surround yourself with beautiful possessions. It should not be forgotten that there is a certain proprietary aspect to the Empress. In fact, one of the first things that should cross your mind when you see this card is the phrase "this is mine."

The Empress and her astrological counterpart, Venus, have a strong leaning towards creativity and the arts, so there will soon be a chance to give your talents an airing. Even if your ambitions do not reach to the dizzying heights of creating a painted masterpiece or composing a stirring symphony, the Empress promises a great deal of pleasure and satisfaction in the very act of creation.

Reversed Meaning:

The maternal nature of the Empress shows a darker side when the card is reversed. It may be that someone is far too protective, allowing loved ones little scope for self-expression. There may be problems that are caused by children who feel frustrated in their home environment. Domestic tyranny and emotional blackmail could be major problems associated with the reversed Empress. There may also be a hint of financial difficulties, and the need to lower one's sights and tighten the belt for a while.

IV (4)

The Emperor

*Alternative Title: The Emperor was called The
Grandfather during the French Revolution.
Esoteric Titles: Son of the Morning, Chief among the
Mighty*

Qabalistic Letter: He, meaning window. Number value 5. Due to Crowley's attribution of the Star to He in his system, the Emperor becomes associated with Tzaddi the fishhook. Number value 90.

Tree of Life Pathway: He represents the fifth pathway between Tiphareth and Chockmah. Tzaddi represents the 18th pathway between Yesod and Netzah.

Direction: Northeast.

Astrological Correspondence:
The first sign of the zodiac, Aries the Ram.

Description:
In most versions of this card, the Emperor sits enthroned wearing an impressive crown. In his right hand he holds a scepter. His left hand sometimes holds an orb or a shield emblazoned with an imperial eagle to show that he is an Emperor rather than a King of the Minor Arcana. It is said that the figure on this card resembles Charlemagne, who was the first Holy Roman Emperor. In the so-called Charles VI deck and the Marseilles Tarot, only the left side of the Emperor's face can be seen, which is reminiscent of the profiles seen on coins. Crowley chose to follow this convention in his Tarot deck but Waite preferred to show the Emperor in full face, seated against a background of high rocky peaks. Both included ram's heads—symbolic of Aries—in their designs.

Symbolism:
The Emperor is the first of the zodiac trump cards and is associated with Aries the Ram, so it shares the characteristics of pioneering energy and fiery potential of that sign. The card, like the sign of the Ram, expresses leadership, dynamism and the assertion of power. Many decks show the Emperor to be dressed in armor. Arms and armor are symbolic of Mars, the Roman god of war, who

is also planetary ruler of the sign of Aries. Ram's heads are often featured on this card.

Just as the Empress is the "Great Mother," so the Emperor is a representation of the "Father God." His mythological progenitors include the Greek Zeus and the Roman Jupiter. This deity, who was known as the "Father of All," ordered the affairs of the gods and men, and he was also considered to be a lusty and indefatigable lover. Thus, the crown of the Emperor represents worldly power, while the scepter in his right hand doubles up as a symbol of power and also a phallic symbol that indicates both virility and fatherhood.

The throne of the Emperor is often cubic in shape (like the plinth of the Devil), showing the foursquare nature of physical reality, and, as it were, symbolizing the real world. Of course, the number four naturally leads us to the four elements, the four seasons, the four cardinal directions as well as the four Gospels and the four cardinal signs of the zodiac. Further descriptions of these symbols can be found throughout the entire Tarot. However, there may be a deeper Qabalistic reason for this fourfold emphasis, because the hidden name of God was said to possess four letters. It was described as the Tetragrammaton or "the four-lettered name." So sacred was this mystery that it was never meant to be spoken aloud or written down. If this was so, one wonders how the knowledge of God's name has been preserved. Be that as it may, the letter He occurs twice in the Tetragrammaton, as it is both the second and fourth letter.

He literally means "window." This is a means of admitting light (knowledge) and air (spirit) into a house. The Emperor is associated with the sense of sight, and so by extension also vision, the ability to analyze, to supervise and to overlook one's domain with vigilance in a protective manner. The letter He also has another connotation. In Hebrew, He is the letter that serves as the Hebrew definite article "the." This word creates precision and it changes the general into the particular, thus defining something and locating it.

Upright Meaning:

The imposing, regal figure of the Emperor represents the fulfillment of ambition. His appearance in a reading can mean one of two things—or both. It may suggest that you have gained the notice of someone of a great power and authority. This person, who is probably male, is well disposed toward you and he will show you favor. Secondly, the card means that you will gain high achievement, honor and renown.

The Emperor is considered to be the card of royalty, but in today's world it represents those who wield power over ordinary people. So, this can represent politicians, employers, managers and administrators. In a woman's reading, the card can represent a strong figure, such as her father or husband, or possibly some other paternal figure in her life in whom she places trust.

In a more general sense, if you have been suffering from a lack of confidence or if you are downhearted, the appearance of the Emperor is a good sign. It indicates that this period of gloom will soon be over. It also indicates that you possess some gift or talent that will enable you to move toward your ultimate goal. In short, the card promises victory, a raising of your status and great honors, but you must remain magnanimous in your hour of triumph. It is also possible that the Emperor of the card refers to yourself. If this is the case, then you will soon have the power to influence events and to emerge well from a crisis, in a position of authority and trust.

Reversed Meaning:

The reversed Emperor can be a real tyrant. His power and authority are implacable and he demands that his will reigns supreme. The paternalism of the upright Emperor now becomes abusive and damaging. Your ambitions will go unfulfilled through the influence of someone who sees you as a threat or who just does not like you or your ideas. If you want to know if someone is trustworthy, the reversed Emperor shows that he is not. If the card appears to indicate part of your own character, then perhaps you are not as strong and capable as you would like others to think.

V (5)

The Hierophant

Alternative Titles: The Pope, The High Priest, Jupiter and
The Priest
Esoteric Title: Magus of the Eternal Gods

Qabalistic Letter: Vau, meaning nail. Number value 6.

Tree of Life Pathway: Sixth, between Chesed and Chockmah.

Direction: Southeast.

Astrological Correspondence:
   This is the second zodiac trump card, and it is associated with Taurus the Bull.

Description:
   In the eyes of a person living in the Middle Ages, there would be no mistaking the central character of this card. The illustration was an obvious depiction of the Pope, an exalted personage as easily recognizable as the Emperor or Empress. He wears clerical vestments and bears the triple tiara of the Papacy on his head. His right hand is raised in the gesture of blessing while his left supports a three-tiered cross. Before him, two (sometimes three) priests or monks kneel in homage. However, official disapproval of the Papal image on the card is such that in some decks it is replaced by the classical figure of thunderbolt wielding Jupiter, or, in at least one pack, by Bacchus, the god of wine and revelry.
   Some modern card designers are also prone to religious embarrassment, so they re-titled the card "The Hierophant"; a term once applied to the High Priest of Eleusis. In addition, the triple tiara has occasionally been replaced by the White Miter of Upper Egypt as worn by the god Osiris, husband of Isis, to symbolically match the new lunar headgear found in "The High Priestess" card.

Symbolism:
   Originally the Hierophant was known as the Pope, the infallible Vicar of Christ, the enthroned supreme Bishop of Rome—and to the medieval mind, the one man on earth who communicated directly with God. One of the titles of the Pope is Pontifex Maximus, the Great Bridge Builder, a name that is an

honor deriving from Roman Emperors. A bridge spans a gap or a river, thus connecting two sides and making communication between them possible.

The Pope is the intermediary between the earthly and the divine. Traditionally his crown and his cross have three levels, and there are usually three characters shown in the card's design. This threefold division is likely to be symbolic of the three basic divisions of the medieval universe: heaven, earth and hell, or to put it in more psychological terms, super-conscious, everyday consciousness and the subconscious.

Discomfort with the use of Roman Catholic symbolism has brought numerous attempts to change the card in some way, sometimes even to the extent of replacing it altogether. For example, the Order of the Golden Dawn preferred to call the card the Hierophant after the High Priest of the annual Eleusian Mysteries, in honor of the goddesses Demeter and Persephone, and this is how the card is most commonly known today.

The Hebrew letter associated with the card is Vau, meaning "nail" or "hook." This word can also be used as "and," which connects two concepts together, just as a bridge does. In this sense the Hierophant can be thought of as a concept that creates a union between the spiritual and the physical. Historically this connection has been made by the use of ritual in religious ceremonies, hence the priestly image on the card.

The Hierophant also links to the sense of hearing, but if one is to hear properly, one must listen in silence. Thus the card also represents quiet and the humble submission to words of greater wisdom and authority.

Upright Meaning:

The Hierophant is a subtle card that often suggests spiritual consolation and wise counsel in times of need. The card represents the higher, idealistic foundations of established religious practices but it can also suggest a teacher or a practical instructor as well as a spiritual guide. If this is so, then an older, more staid individual is indicated.

When this card appears in a reading, it may well be the case that you will encounter someone who will fulfill the role of personal guru, although this is unusual. It is more common for the card to refer to a set of events occurring around you that will provide their own lessons in moral and spiritual guidance.

In essence, the Hierophant represents the capacity to tell right from wrong and good from bad. It signifies the telltale signs of both good and bad, which allows you to make the correct decisions. It also indicates the tried and true, the proper way to behave and the values of traditional moral virtues. So, if your question involves a novel concept as opposed to an old fashioned and accepted mode of thought, then the answer of the Hierophant is that conventionality is the correct route at this time.

The Hierophant is a traditional indicator of marriage. If a less formal, more modern relationship is being considered, then the appearance of this card shows that there will be outside pressure to make the union more conventional. The card can also point to contractual obligations, legal responsibilities and signing official documents.

Reversed Meaning:

When the Hierophant is reversed, the moral judgments and opinions of others usually play too great a role. In this negative position it often indicates looking and judging. There is the possibility that hidebound tradition is holding you back, stifling your individuality and stopping you from being the person that you truly are. The card may also reveal a crisis of faith that manifests as uncharacteristic behavior and disorderly conduct.

However, the reversed Hierophant does have a message that is possibly more positive now than it would have been even a century ago; it could conceivably mean rejecting bad advice, or making your own decisions in defiance of an outworn value system.

VI (6)

The Lovers

Alternative Title: The Lover
Esoteric Titles: Children of the Voice Divine, Oracles of the Mighty Gods

Qabalistic Letter: Zain, meaning sword or penis. Number value 7.

Tree of Life Pathway: Seventh, between Tiphareth and Binah.

Direction: East (above).

Astrological Correspondence:
The Lovers card is associated with the zodiac sign of Gemini the Twins.

Description:
This card varies in design more than any other, with the possible exception of Judgement. In the traditional "Marseilles" version, a young man stands between two women. His body inclines toward one while his head turns to face the other. Overhead the figure of Cupid, god of love, is about to loose his arrow of desire. One very early Tarot deck shows several sets of lovers promenading, while above them two Cupids on a cloud take aim.

A. E. Waite completely changed the card design. In his version, Cupid becomes the powerful central figure of the archangel Raphael. The setting is the Garden of Eden with Adam standing on the right in front of the Tree of Life, while Eve, apple of temptation in hand, stands on the left before the Tree of Knowledge, which has a serpent crawling up it. Between the two humans and their respective trees, a solitary mountain peak rears in the distance.

Symbolism:
Crowley viewed the card as a mystical union and claimed that, in keeping with the true symbolism of the card, it should have been entitled "The Brothers," proclaiming that the original, lost card design showed the struggle between Cain and Able. His reasoning was probably based on the fact that this card is allocated to Gemini the Twins.

Waite's version is full of symbolic detail. The Tree of Life behind Adam has twelve trefoils, signifying the signs of the zodiac and their decans. The Tree of Knowledge of Good and Evil behind Eve bears five fruits representing the five senses. The archangel Raphael symbolizes heavenly wisdom or the "super-conscious mind," which is partly concealed by clouds of worldly ignorance.

The traditional card design is probably a depiction of a classical theme, which is the judgment of Paris. According to the story, which is a preliminary to Homer's epic of the fall of Troy, the gods were forced to choose which goddess was the most beautiful, and the prize for this accolade was to be a golden apple. Preferring to avoid responsibility, they decided that a mortal should make the choice. So three goddesses, Hera, Athena and Aphrodite appeared before Paris, the prince of Troy. Each offered the young man a bribe; Hera, the queen of Olympus, promised him power if he would choose her, while Athena's incentive came in the form of wisdom. However, there was clearly no contest, because Aphrodite (Venus) showed Paris a vision of the most beautiful woman in the world, Helen. When she promised that Helen would be his, he was overwhelmed by love and immediately awarded the contest to Aphrodite, proclaiming her to be the most beautiful of goddesses. Hera and Athena were greatly put out and swore that trouble would follow; they were right, the trouble turned out to be the ten-year long Trojan war.

The Hebrew letter associated with the Lovers is Zain, meaning "sword." It can also carry the connotation of the penis or of penetration. In Tarot terms, the sword is associated with the mind and the faculty of logical reasoning. It therefore implies choice, a division between decisions that are made with the heart and the head. It is also interesting to note that Adam and Eve were expelled from the Garden by an angel with a sword.

Upright Meaning:

The literal interpretation of the Lovers involves affairs of the heart. In many cases, the appearance of this card suggests that a new amorous adventure is in the offing. A new lover, a new relationship and deep emotional commitment are indicated. Even if matters such as this are furthest from your mind, you will be surprised by the intensity of feeling that is to come.

In a more general sense, the Lovers card reveals that the time has come to make an important decision that will affect the rest of your life. There may be a conflict between your duty and your heart's true desire. This is an important matter, because two paths lie before you. One of these involves taking a great risk, but the advantage of this is that you could gain great happiness and emotional fulfillment. The other path is far more conventional, as it promises to continue your way of life as is usual for you. The advantage of this path is safety and previously established security. The first way offers excitement and the other a calm, ordered pattern of life—one with which you will inevitably become bored in the long run.

It seems that in the choice between these two radically different courses, logic does not play much of a role. It is the heart that should speak and dominate the issue, so follow your feelings, because happiness will follow.

On a less profound note, the Lovers card can also show the establishment of a very close friendship that touches you deeply.

Reversed Meaning:

An unfulfilling life, an unhappy love affair and dissatisfaction with the status quo are shown when the Lovers are reversed. Your devotion to duty may blight your chances of personal happiness. The choice of lifestyle indicated by the upright card is still before you, but there may be a lack of courage and commitment on your part to take that step. There may be a separation from a lover when the card is in this position, however this is not necessarily a permanent situation, even though it will be an unwelcome development.

VII (7)

The Chariot

*Alternative Titles: The Wagon, The Triumphal Chariot,
The Cart, Mastery*
*Esoteric Titles: Child of the Power of Waters, Lord of the
Triumph of Light*

Qabalistic Letter: Cheth, meaning fence or enclosure. Number value 8.

Tree of Life Pathway: Eighth, between Geburah and Binah.

Direction: East (below).

Astrological Correspondence:
The zodiac sign of Cancer the Crab.

Description:
In the fifteenth-century Tarot deck designed by Bonifacio Bembo, the Chariot card shows a queen riding in a chariot drawn by two white horses. Equally unusual is an old Florentine pack depicting a child precariously perched high on his triumphal cart. The babe holds two placards, on which are written Fama (fame) and Vola (will). However, the usual image for this card is that of a conquering hero, crowned and victorious, standing in a chariot beneath a canopy. Indeed this is the image that has been preserved in most modern Tarot decks. The only significant alteration to this design that has occurred is the occasional tendency to replace the horses with Egyptian sphinxes as in the A. E. Waite pack. Aleister Crowley went even further, providing his fully armored golden hero with four sphinx-like steeds, possessing the heads of a bull, an eagle, a human and a lion (see The Wheel of Fortune and The World) as well as the crest of a crab referring to the card's astrological correspondence.

Symbolism:
The tradition of the victory parade goes back at least to the early days of the Roman Empire, when a conquering hero would ride in his chariot through the streets of the capital, followed by his legions and cartloads of booty. This was known as a Triumph, the very origin of the word Trump, meaning a card of the Major Arcana. The Romans added one twist to this ceremony of self-

glorification by positioning a slave in the rear of the chariot. The slave not only held a crown above the head of the victor but also whispered in his ear the words, "Look not so proud, for the gods are jealous," a warning against the greatest sin against the Olympian deities, that of hubris or overweening vanity. However, in the Tarot, the charioteer is usually crowned and there is no one to warn him against the dangers of arrogance.

The identity of this proud and youthful charioteer is in dispute. In the versions where he is armored, it is easy to equate this figure with Mars, god of war, but it should also be remembered that in Greek and Roman mythology, Helios (or Apollo), the sun god, also rode in a chariot across the heavens each day. One story tells of how Phaeton, the son of Helios, begged his father to let him drive the sun chariot just once. After much persuasion Helios yielded and allowed his headstrong son to take the reins. Disaster followed, as vast areas of the earth's surface were blasted by solar heat while others froze in terrible night. To save the universe, Zeus/Jupiter cast a thunderbolt at Phaeton knocking him from the chariot to fall to his death far below.

The solar symbolism of the card is reinforced by its astrological correspondence with the sign of Cancer the crab. Although this sign is ruled by the moon, it actually begins at the summer solstice when the sun is at its strongest, and which is the longest day of the year in the Northern Hemisphere. This is indeed "The Lord of the Triumph of Light."

There is a Cancerian aspect to the Qabalistic symbolism, too. The Hebrew letter Cheth, meaning a "fence" or "enclosure," is reminiscent of the shell of a crab. The Chariot itself can be regarded as a moveable fence, protecting the youthful occupant. The same might be said of his golden armor.

Upright Meaning:

This card represents the "vehicle" of one's self-expression. It is the means by which we make progress in this world. The armor of the charioteer suggests that there are battles to be fought and inner strength will be needed to overcome the forces that stand against you. The odd thing is that this is unlikely to come as a surprise to you, because the card suggests that this struggle has been going on for a while and the Chariot in a reading encourages you to continue, as the contest is likely to be ongoing.

The Chariot shows that you are the master of your own fortunes and that you can point your life in the right direction. In keeping with the triumphal symbolism, the card may also be taken as a warning against being too smug or taking excessive pride in your achievements. Remember to act with humility.

On a more mundane note, the Chariot can often be taken literally as a vehicle of some kind. It may be that you will purchase a new vehicle or undertake a journey. If the card does represent travel then it is likely that the journey will relate to duty and work rather than purely for pleasure.

Reversed Meaning:

The arrogance implied by the card becomes quite forceful when it is reversed. An over-inflated ego may be indicated and you may be trumpeting your own self-importance far too much. The reversed Chariot can also indicate frustration, because you think that things are not moving quickly enough to suit you. You may also feel pressurized and prone to childish outbursts and fits of temper that are directed against those who do not deserve your wrath.

You may feel that your life is not going in the direction that you want it to. There are obstacles in your path and seemingly endless delays. Travel plans are likely to be a headache. Perhaps some soothing meditative techniques would help your frame of mind when the Chariot is found in the reversed position.

VIII (8)

Strength

*This card is number eight according to the Golden
Dawn/Crowley system. In more traditional decks this card
is numbered XI (11).*
*Alternative Titles: Fortitude, Force, Lust and the
Enchantress*
*Esoteric Titles: Daughter of the Flaming Sword, Leader of
the Lion*

Qabalistic Letter: Teth, meaning serpent. Number value 9.

Tree of Life Pathway: Ninth, between Geburah and Chesed.

Direction: North (above).

Astrological Correspondence:
The obvious association of this card is with the zodiac sign of Leo the Lion.

Description:
In most Tarot decks a female figure gently but firmly holds a lion by the jaws. In most old decks this lady wears a large, floppy hat reminiscent of that worn by the Magician. However, in one of the oldest decks that was once thought to have been designed by Jacques Gringonneur for mad King Charles VI of France, a seated woman effortlessly breaks a pillar in two.

Most designers have preferred a more conventional image of strength, such as that of Hercules armed with a club defeating the Nemean Lion, which was the first of his famous Labors. Aleister Crowley, on the other hand, once again departed from convention with his version of the card. He had no trouble identifying the mysterious lady with Babalon (sic), "Mother of Abominations" from the Book of Revelations, otherwise known as the Scarlet Woman raising a goblet containing the blood of saints. In the Crowley design (actually executed by Lady Frieda Harris) the lion becomes the Great Beast of the Apocalypse (in other words Crowley's view of himself), complete with seven heads and ten horns as in the Biblical description. To complete this radical new image, Crowley re-titled the card "Lust."

Symbolism:
Strength is one of the three named virtues in the Major Arcana of the Tarot. The most obvious, if slightly obscure origin of the image of a woman wrestling with a lion, is the Greek myth of the

nymph Cyrene, a follower of the lunar huntress-goddess Artemis. One day Cyrene was contending with a lion when the god Apollo, the solar twin brother of Artemis, spied her. Apollo immediately took a fancy to this brave girl and made her his lover.

The Hebrew letter assigned to this card is Teth, meaning "serpent." The letter itself even looks like a snake. The serpent, like the lion, is also a symbol of strength and this turns up in many different roles in the myths and religious beliefs of most societies. Primarily it is associated with immortality and rejuvenation because it sheds its skin. It is also a phallic symbol, like the club of Hercules or the pillar, in many versions of this card. Because snakes live under rocks or in holes, they are symbolically connected to the underworld, to the dead, to fertility and to the unconscious mind. In Christian terms, the serpent is a symbol of evil because it tempted Eve in the Garden of Eden. However, in astrological terms, the sign of the serpent is actually the sigil of Leo the lion.

The lion itself is obviously connected to the sign of Leo and is the symbol of strength, grace, majesty and leadership. The woman of the card either closes or opens the lion's mouth, symbolizing the control over the savage, baser instincts and perhaps more importantly, the control over speech.

Cyrene's floppy hat is shaped like that of the Magician, in a figure of eight. This is the symbol of eternity, signifying dominion, wisdom and magical power.

Upright Meaning:

The image of Strength in this card can refer to physical strength, yet it does not imply feats of endurance or great heroic deeds. Willpower, tenacity, self-belief and mental resilience are fundamental to this card. It can be interpreted as the ability to withstand enormous pressures and overcome them.

Forget your insecurities because you have challenges to face, obstacles to overcome and enemies to defeat. So do not begin your struggle by fighting yourself first. You know what to do, and it is the right thing. Do not shy away from it. This is your chance to prove yourself and improve your own self-esteem at the same time.

The card is a very welcome addition to any reading if one has been ill, because it is a sure indicator of a rapid recovery. Another side to the card is connected to overcoming bad habits. So, if you are a smoker, then Strength can show that you have the necessary willpower to overcome your habit.

If health matters are not issues, then Strength indicates fighting for what is right. If the card does foretell a battle then it is one that you are well equipped to win. You are up to the challenge and your courage and determination will ensure your victory. You will defeat ignorance and oppression, triumph over spiteful and envious people and you can be sure that you are doing the right thing. Just remember to reward yourself when the struggle is over.

Reversed Meaning:

The determination of the upright Strength may be completely misplaced when the card is reversed. You may be pursuing the wrong goal entirely. On the other hand, this could be an indication of cowardice, losing one's nerve and giving in just when victory is in sight. You may have to fight with yourself or to rely on someone else to provide the backbone you desperately need in a time of challenge. Even so, you are still about to take the lead, even if it is only as a figurehead.

IX (9)

The Hermit

*Alternative Titles: The Monk, The Old Man, The Veiled
Lamp, The Wise One, The Traitor*
*Esoteric Titles: Magus of the Voice of Light, Prophet of the
Gods*

Qabalistic Letter: Yod, meaning hand. Number value 10.

Tree of Life Pathway: Tenth, between Chesed and Tiphareth.

Direction: North (below).

Astrological Correspondence:
   The Hermit is associated with the zodiac sign of Virgo the Virgin.

Description:
   The design of the Hermit card varies little between one deck and another. A solitary old man with a long, white beard is dressed somewhat like a friar or wandering monk bearing a staff. This gives the general impression of a penitent on pilgrimage. In the Tarot designs for the James Bond film "Live and Let Die" (1973), the aged Hermit is shown sitting on a rock surrounded by the sea. However, in most card designs the Hermit holds a lamp, its feeble glimmer providing the only light. Often the monk shields the lamp's wan flame with his cloak. In the Waite version of the card, the Hermit stands on a cold, snowy mountain peak holding his lamp aloft. Actually, the Hermit's lamp may be a rendering of an hourglass indicating the passage of time.

Symbolism:
   Although Mathers and his adepts of the Golden Dawn allocate this card to the sign of Virgo, the actual image here is a common medieval one of Saturn, signifying old age and infirmity. The hourglass expresses the passage of time, its dim light being the failing life force itself. This is the first time that Saturn, the lord of the passage of inexorable time, makes his appearance in the Major Arcana of the Tarot. He turns up again in the cards of Death, The Devil and The World (only the last is actually allocated to him in the Golden Dawn system).

It has been suggested that the Hermit, carefully feeling his way through darkness, is the "lost" virtue of the Tarot. The classical virtues are four in number, being Justice, Strength, Temperance and Prudence. The first three are represented as cards, but where is the fourth, Prudence? The Hermit card does fit the bill to some extent. The card is associated with the sign of Virgo and therefore with the attributes of that sign—which are caution, thoughtfulness and a prudent attitude to life and its problems. It should not be forgotten that Virgo is a virgin, as indeed we assume the aged monk of the card to be. The walking staff in the Hermit's hand is a symbol of Mercury, the archetypal traveler. Mercury is the ruling planet of Virgo.

The number of the card is nine, the trinity of trinities and therefore the last of the single digits. This may also point to the ninth month, September, which begins within the sign of Virgo. In Jewish tradition Virgo falls within the month of Elul, the time of preparation for the "Days of Awe." This period should be spent in inner reflection and assessing the sincerity of our motives. It is basic arithmetic to associate nine with eighteen, the number of the Moon. So the Hermit may be thought of as passing through the dread landscape of that desolate and disturbing card.

The Hebrew letter connected with the Hermit is Yod. Yod is seen as the "command letter," because all of the letters of the Hebrew alphabet are constructed from Yod shapes. The Yod is always found at the top, symbolically connected to heaven. Yod literally means "hand;" in this case an open hand, as opposed to Kaph, which means "cupped hand" (see The Wheel of Fortune). However Yod can also refer to sex and to seed. This is an odd connection in the light of the association with the sign of the virgin. The number value of Yod is ten, which by the rules of numerology returns us to 1, the first path, the road of the Fool of card 0. Therefore the Hermit can be seen as an aspect of this original traveler, now careworn, burdened by age and who has become a possessor of great wisdom and experience. Alternatively, this can be seen as yet another connection to Mercury by linking the Hermit to the Magician, card 1.

Upright Meaning:

The Hermit is obviously connected to solitude and deep thought, although this need not necessarily imply a withdrawal from the company of others. It may be that you are prone to deep reflection even when surrounded by people, that this is an inner process rather than one found in the outside world. On the other hand, you may feel the need to live quietly for a while to give you the opportunity to put your thoughts in order. Whenever this card turns up, there will be a slowing down of events, the need for patience and the chance of a rethink. Any delays that the card foretells are necessary ones that must be borne with calm acceptance. After all, this card may show that you are being prevented from making a serious error. You can now weigh your options and think things through in a cool, calm and deliberate frame of mind.

The card is also connected to old age and the wisdom that is gained through experience. It may indicate a passage of time, revealing that whatever you have on your mind will take a while before it is resolved. Equally, the card may stand for caution, so it advises you to develop a prudent attitude, to take your time and not be pressured or to rush into anything.

The Hermit card reveals that there is always something new to learn, and this lesson may come from the experiences of someone who has maturity and wisdom on their side. If your question concerns health issues, then the Hermit indicates a time of convalescence.

Reversed Meaning:

Impatience and rash folly are shown when the card is reversed. You may feel lonely and isolated, possibly as a result of a betrayal. Conversely, you may become youthfully arrogant and dismissive of the past and tradition. The reversed Hermit may also show the cantankerous obstinacy usually associated with old age, showing up in the character of someone of any vintage. There may also be forgetfulness and a petulant refusal of any help that may be offered.

X (10)

The Wheel of Fortune

Alternative Title: The Wheel
Esoteric Title: Lord of the Forces of Life

Qabalistic Letter: Kaph, meaning hand or cup—possibly cupped hand. Number value 20.

Tree of Life Pathway: Eleventh, between Hesed and Netzah.

Direction: West.

Astrological Correspondence:

The Wheel of Fortune is associated with the planet Jupiter.

Description:

Apart from the central image of the Wheel itself, this card shows considerable variation between individual Tarot decks. Some very early examples show the blindfolded goddess "Fortune," otherwise known as "Lady Luck," turning a lever operating the Wheel; in others, this fickle deity sits at the hub of the Wheel, which revolves around her. Human figures desperately hang on to the rim. On one side a man is ascending, reaching out for higher position, while on the other side a figure fearfully clutches the Wheel as he descends. At the bottom of the Wheel beneath Fortune, is the wretched figure of a man who has fallen from the Wheel. Above, either a crowned king with the ears of an ass is precariously perched, or a crowned monkey mocks at human pretensions. Other interesting features found in some old decks are the labels that issue from the mouths of these characters. These translate as "I have ruled," "I rule" and "I will rule." The Wheel itself and the blind Lady Luck are "Without rule." More modern Tarot decks tend to depict several strange creatures hanging onto the wheel's rim. One of them is a baboon, which ascends; another is a weird composite creature that falls and finally, a sphinx that sits smugly at the top.

Symbolism:

The Wheel is an archetypal symbol for the vagaries of fate or "the slings and arrows of outrageous fortune." In many ancient mythologies, the goddesses of fate were pictured as weaving the web of human destinies on a loom or spinning wheel. In more modern terms, the spin of a roulette wheel is a similar arbiter of fortune.

In versions of the card that have human figures clinging to the wheel, the symbolism is self-explanatory. However, when the riders of the wheel are depicted as animals, they can present a mystery. The ascending baboon can be taken as a symbol of the Egyptian god Thoth, or his classical equivalent, Mercury, who was considered to be the fast thinking wheeler-dealer. The strange creature that is falling is also symbolic of an Egyptian god, in this case, Set the evildoer, the lord of the desert storm and murderer of his brother.

The sphinx, which sits on top of the Wheel, in common with the sphinxes of the Chariot, possessed all the attributes of the four fixed signs of the zodiac—Aquarius, Scorpio (here an eagle rather than the more familiar scorpion), Leo and Taurus. This is because the mythological creature possesses the head of a man, the wings of an eagle, the body of a lion and the tail of a bull. These symbols can also stand for the four directions, the four seasons, the four elements and even the four Biblical Disciples, Luke, John, Mark and Matthew in that order. These symbols occur again, albeit in a slightly different form, in the World card.

The Wheel is another candidate for the "lost" Tarot virtue of Prudence (see The Hermit). The reasoning behind this goes as follows: as has been previously stated, there are four classical virtues, namely Justice, Strength, Temperance and Prudence. Each of the virtues that appear in the Major Arcana possesses an attribute of the suits of the Minor Arcana. Justice holds a Sword, Temperance two Cups, some versions of Strength show a Club, so, logically Prudence should include a Coin. Thus the Wheel is identified as Prudence, however the same logic would also lead to the Hanged Man, who sometimes has coins falling from his pockets.

The Wheel is also associated with the planet Jupiter and the Hebrew letter Kaph. According to myth, Jupiter sought to distract the three fate goddesses by talking to them while they spun, so that destiny would turn out more to his liking. Kaph expresses the idea of the cupped hand or a hand concealing its contents. It also connects to grasping, both in a physical sense and also the metaphorical sense, such as comprehending an idea. In this case, the concepts to be grasped are the mysterious actions of fate itself.

Upright Meaning:

This card indicates a stroke of luck. The Wheel is spinning for you, and your life will take a turn for the better. You will be riding high for a while, but you need to bear in mind that it is fate that has taken a hand in your affairs and given you a gift, so don't start patting yourself on the back just yet. Whether upright or reversed, the Wheel indicates a temporary phase in life. If you are prudent, you will use this period of excellent luck to put something away for a time when things will become more difficult. It is important to bear in mind that this is a Wheel, and you, like the human or animal figures, are on its rim. Now you go up, but one day the Wheel will spin again and you may not be so lucky.

Good luck signals the start of this period. You may find lost coins or an uncashed check. Take note of the area in a reading where this card occurs, because this will be the area where your luck will come from.

Reversed Meaning:

There could a few unpleasant surprises when the Wheel is reversed. Constant ups and downs in fortune will tend to confuse you, but remember it is the nature of the Wheel to turn, and this upsetting period will not last forever.

XI (11)

Justice

In traditional decks, the Justice card is numbered VIII (8), but according to the Golden Dawn/Crowley system it is numbered XI (11).
Alternative Title: Adjustment
Esoteric Titles: Daughter of the Lord of Truth, Holder of the Balances

Qabalistic Letter: Lamed, meaning ox-goad or whip. Number value 30.

Tree of Life Pathway: Thirty, between Tiphareth and Geburah.

Direction: Northwest.

Astrological Correspondence:
 The zodiac sign of Libra the Scales.

Description:
 The familiar female figure of Justice sits enthroned, usually crowned with a heraldic "mural" crown resembling castle battlements. This type of headgear is mostly associated with towns and cities and therefore "civilization" in the widest sense. In the Tarot system, Justice is rarely if ever blind, because in traditional renderings of the card, she lacks her blindfold, gazing boldly into the eyes of the viewer. As is to be expected, she holds the balance of fairness and equilibrium in one hand while the other grasps the sword of retribution and severity.

Symbolism:
 Justice is one of the four Tarot virtues, the others being Temperance, Strength and the concealed Prudence. The symbolism of the Justice card is intimately mingled with that of the zodiac sign of Libra. The zodiac sign of the Balances begins at the autumnal equinox in late September, and at this time the hours of light and darkness are equal. In the first century A.D. the Roman poet Manilius wrote, "Day and night are weighed in Libra's scales, equal awhile at last the night prevails."

 A figure representing Justice is one of the oldest human symbols. In Ancient Egypt, this force of rightness and impartiality was identified as the goddess Maat, who signified the universal order. Maat was shown wearing a single feather in her headdress, and this feather came to represent purity of thought and motive. In the Egyptian Book of the Dead, the heart (symbolizing the soul or true identity) was shown being weighed against the feather of truth.

The Greeks and Romans personified Justice as the wise goddess, Themis, who occupied the middle ground, being dignified and impartial, giving her advice to all who required it.

When Mathers placed this card at the eleventh position within the Major Arcana, he placed Justice at the heart of the Tarot exactly half way in the sequence of cards. The symbolism of the scales is self evident, while the sword represents the intelligence to cut through any argument, as well as the capacity to punish wrongdoing. This echoes the nature of the suit of Swords in the Minor Arcana.

In Qabalistic terms, the letter Lamed means the "ox-goad" or "whip." In other words, Lamed urges and corrects the behavior of the ox. The ox is represented by the letter Aleph or the Fool card.

Upright Meaning:

The meaning of this card is obvious, because it means justice, pure and simple. It relates to the concepts of logic, fairness, equilibrium and impartiality in thought and deed, and a just attitude in all dealings with others. The use of reason and a cool exercise of the intellect will usually provide the answers to your questions when Justice appears in your reading. The Justice card points the way to giving and receiving fair advice. When upright, this also indicates that the judgments of powerful people will work in your favor. It also denotes that this is only right and proper, because you justly deserve the rewards that influential people can bestow upon you.

The Justice card indicates an inner balance of a cool and rational kind. Legal issues may be highlighted, as would contracts that will be equitable and beneficial to you, or possibly a court case, which will be found in your favor. In short, Justice shows success in all legal affairs and the probability of business proposals that will work to your advantage. The upright Justice card can show the righting of a wrong that has been done to you in the past. It may even indicate a personal crusade to see justice done on behalf of someone else. It highlights issues of honesty, loyalty and idealism.

On a more spiritual level, Justice can be seen as the working out of positive karma. You could be rewarded for good deeds that you have done in the past. So, a run of particularly good luck is to be expected as the cosmic balance rights itself in your favor.

The connection to the sign of Libra is also taken into consideration in the card's interpretation. The sign is intimately connected to marriage, business partnership and indeed any relationship that stands the test of time. The appearance of the Justice card is extremely fortuitous for all these important matters.

Reversed Meaning:

Justice in both upright and reversed positions insists that a cool, calm, intellectual attitude will help you and your situation. When reversed, the card provides a warning. Take care, think things through carefully, perhaps more than once, otherwise the forces that are ranged against you will do you harm.

The reversed Justice literally has the opposite meaning to its upright position. It is usually interpreted as injustice, decisions going against you even if you are morally in the right. Legal affairs tend to be particularly troublesome. False accusations may be made against you and you could conceivably encounter some form of oppression or prejudice. Misinformation given to you through malice or simple misunderstanding can be very damaging. The reversed Justice card also shows self-seeking advisors, and you would be wise to choose your confidants with great care.

If you are considering signing a contract or entering into a legal dispute when the reversed Justice appears, then think again. The trials and tribulations that you will go through will not be worth the effort and will tend to blight your life in some way.

I have noticed that when the upright Justice card appears, it doesn't necessarily mean that the person will get everything that he wants from a situation, but that what he does get will be fair and just.

XII (12)

The Hanged Man

Alternative Titles: The Lone Man, Judas
Esoteric Title: Spirit of the Mighty Waters

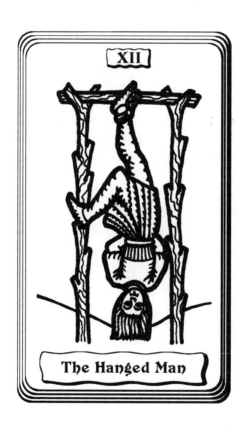

Qabalistic Letter: Mem, meaning the sea. Number value 40.

Tree of Life Pathway: Thirteenth, between Hod and Geburah.

Direction: East to West.

Astrological Correspondence:

Traditionally, this card is ascribed to the element of Water. In recent times it has also become associated with the planet Neptune.

Description:

This is undoubtedly the strangest card in the deck. In fact, it is so odd that it has become virtually synonymous with the Tarot itself. The image portrayed here is one of a particularly nasty medieval punishment called "bafflement" in which the unfortunate offender would be hung upside down, often until death. In the so-called Charles VI Tarot deck, the Hanged Man is shown dangling from a scaffold reminiscent of a doorway. In this card design, his hands are free to hold two sacks of coins. Most other versions of the card retain the roughly cut doorway, but place the Hanged Man with his legs crossed and his arms behind his back in a pose that resembles a downward pointed arrow. Sometimes coins are shown falling from the hanging victim. A.E. Waite preferred to hang the poor man from a T-shaped cross, while Aleister Crowley not only suspends his faceless figure from an Ankh (the ancient Egyptian symbol of life) but also manages to crucify him on the Qabalistic Tree of Life itself. Although some versions of this card show the Hanged Man to be in torment, most show him smiling as if contented with his strange fate.

Symbolism:

Many modern commentators on this card seem convinced that the origin of this unique image can be found in an ancient Nordic saga called the "Lay of the High One." In this mythological poem, the dark, shamanic god Odin puts himself through a terrible ordeal by hanging from the World-Tree Yggdrasil for nine days and nights in order to win the secret of the mysterious Runes. However, I find this connection between the Runes and the Tarot extremely tenuous, if only because it has never once been suggested that Odin hung himself upside down.

It has also been suggested that the dangling figure is Judas, who hanged himself out of remorse for his betrayal of Christ. The coins sometimes seen falling from the Hanged Man are taken to be the thirty pieces of silver that Judas was paid for his treachery. The same objection applies to this identification, too. There has never been any suggestion that Judas chose to commit suicide by hanging himself by his foot.

Antoine de Court de Gebelin thought that the image was nothing more than a printer's error and that the card actually represented the Tarot's missing virtue, Prudence (the other three are Strength, Justice and Temperance). The young man stands on one leg while carefully considering his next step. However since the very earliest Tarot decks were hand-drawn rather than printed, this too seems very unlikely. So, we are left with a mystery that probably never will be fully explained.

On a more symbolic note, the card is numbered twelve, the number of signs in the zodiac and therefore the end of the cycle and the beginning of the next. It is associated with the Water element and the planet Neptune. Its Hebrew letter is Mem, meaning the sea, waters or oceans. The last sign of the zodiac is Pisces the Fish; a Water sign ruled by Neptune associated with the concepts of self-sacrifice and mystical awareness, and also with imprisonment and punishment.

Upright Meaning:

This card turns the world on its head. It indicates a reversal of values, self-sacrifice, spiritual rather than material benefits and much confusion. The Hanged Man can indicate a temporary reversal of fortunes; a karmic debt that must be paid before you can move on and make the most of life. It may be that you have been looking at things the wrong way and this is the time to change your perspective. You may feel as though you are out of control, being pushed around and generally taken advantage of. This may be so, but it is advisable to grin and bear it for a while, because any attempt to change the situation would be a complete waste of time and effort. On the other hand, you can be sure that this whole process is a rapid learning curve and you will ultimately benefit from the lessons you are receiving.

The card shows a passive phase and being forced to be patient. Sometimes this card can quite literally indicate a period of illness and recuperation. The Hanged Man can also show a trial of passage as you move from one phase of life to another, increasing your spiritual awareness as you do so.

Reversed Meaning:

When reversed, the Hanged Man looks as though he were standing on one leg, which is tethered to the spot. This may indicate that there is a strong desire to move on, but an inability to let go of the past. There is a possibility that you are being manipulated by people who are using emotional blackmail for their interest rather than yours. On the other hand, it may be that you yourself are playing the part of a martyr. Perhaps you feel a burden of guilt for some past real or imagined misdemeanor. Ask yourself whether you are punishing yourself for something that was not your fault. Only when you can remove this misplaced masochistic kind of self-blame will you be free to move on.

XIII (13)

Death

Alternative Titles: Mortality, Transformation, the Reaper
The card is also sometimes left tactfully untitled.
Esoteric Title: Child of the Great Transformers, Lord of
the Gates of Death

Qabalistic Letter: Nun, meaning fish. If Nun is used as a verb then it means "to sprout" or "to grow." Number value 50.

Tree of Life Pathway: Fourteenth, between Netzah and Tiphareth.

Direction: Southwest (in Hindu belief this is the direction of Nirriti, the goddess of nightmares).

Astrological Correspondence:

The card is associated with the sign of Scorpio, "Oh death, where is thy sting, oh grave thy victory?"

Description:

The menacing figure of skeletal Death, the "Grim Reaper" strides across a desolate landscape in most Tarot decks. Around this ghastly apparition are heads, hands and other body parts as well as discarded symbols of power and prestige such as crowns and coins, signifying that death is the "Great Leveler," because all are equal before his scythe. In some decks there is a river in the background symbolizing the Jordan or the mythical Styx, which was the Underworld stream. A setting sun sinks below the distant horizon. In several versions of the card, most notably that of A. E. Waite, Death is shown in black armor riding on a pale horse, as death is described in the Book of Revelations. People from all walks of life: kings, bishops, merchants and peasants, young and old vainly beg this implacable specter for mercy.

In Waite's design, Death lacks his usual scythe, instead bearing a banner emblazoned with a white heraldic rose symbolizing new life or perhaps life in the face of death. The rose may represent hope but it is a fragile bloom, which once removed from its parent plant begins to die, albeit retaining its beauty until the last petal falls.

Symbolism:

The first recognizable Tarot cards that we know of appeared in Europe in the early fifteenth century. At this period the Black

Death, which was a bubonic plague epidemic of cataclysmic proportions, had swept across Asia and Europe, wiping out at the very least one third of the entire population of those lands. Many of the grief-stricken survivors firmly believed that the onset of this terrible disease signaled the "last days," which are the preliminary to the end of the world. A morbid artistic theme became apparent in the art of the time. This was "The Dance of Death" or the "Danse Macabre," which was a composition showing grinning skeletons, seen to be reveling in the misfortunes of suffering humanity. So it is not surprising that the menacing presence of the Grim Reaper makes his appearance combined with the unlucky number 13 in the Major Arcana of the Tarot.

The clue to the origin of this skeletal personification of Death may lie with his primary attribute, which is the scythe. The scythe, sickle or reaping hook was symbolic of the Roman deity Saturn, and his ancient Greek equivalent Chronos, the god of time. Today, this personage is best known as "Old Father Time" when he makes his annual appearance at New Year. However, he wore a darker face when he symbolized the old Celtic New Year, which is now the modern festival of Halloween.

In Qabalistic terms, the associated Hebrew letter Nun means "fish." This is interesting, because even today we tend to see more dead fish than we see live ones. When a fish leaves the water it is removed from its own aquatic world and it will inevitably expire. On the other hand, when used as a verb, Nun means "to grow" or "to sprout," thus indicating new life to replace that which has passed. Nun can also be used as a euphemism for the fish-like spermatozoa which bring us to the orgasm—or as Victorians were fond of referring to it, the Little Death. The link between sex and death is deeply ingrained in human psychology. This link is also strongly connected to the symbolism of the card's astrological correspondence with the mysterious and sometimes sinister zodiac sign of Scorpio.

The scorpion is regarded as the swift and sly dealer of death and is therefore a perfect correspondence for this card. Those born under the sign are considered to be very sexy, intense and vengeful with a proverbial "sting in the tail."

Upright Meaning:

The unwelcome appearance of the grinning Death in a card reading is likely to cause distress, yet its primary interpretation isn't usually as sinister as this ghastly apparition would imply. There is no doubt that once, when life was uncertain, brutish and likely to be brief, the Death card meant exactly that—physical death! Indeed the card can still mean death, but I must emphasize that this interpretation is the exception rather than the rule. In this day and age it is more likely to indicate an irrevocable ending—a death of sorts, but this should be taken in a broader sense, such as the passing of a way of life, a relationship, outdated attitudes or a job. The change may be shocking and unpleasant, yet it will serve to sweep away the outmoded, and will ultimately prove to be a blessing in disguise. The old and restrictive are consigned to the garbage cans of history and a new beginning is about to dawn. Remember that the skeleton is the most resilient part of the physical structure and it remains long after the weak flesh is gone. Likewise, the underlying truth remains even when all else is stripped away, because the Death card leaves no room for illusions of any sort. It represents the ultimate reality.

Reversed Meaning:

The reversed meaning of the Death card is little different from the upright, however there is a more fearful edge to the card because you may view any changes with horror and be afflicted with extremes of anxiety. There is, paradoxically a more positive aspect to the reversed card, because frightening as it may be, fate seems to be just a little more flexible, because it gives you more control over your own destiny. It is true that an ending must come, but you will be in a position to decide exactly when and how.

I have noticed time and again when this card appears in a spread that it shows that something is at or has come to a complete end. If a client is clinging to the hope that a lover will come back or that a dying marriage, a dying business or any other dead or dying situation will revive, it just won't do so. The end really is the end in this case, and it is time for the person to move on and open the door to something new.

XIV (14)

Temperance

Alternative Titles: Art, The Guide
Esoteric Titles: Daughter of the Reconcilers, Bringer
Forth of Life

Qabalistic Letter: Samekh, meaning crutch, support or tent peg. Number value 60.

Tree of Life Pathway: Fifteenth, between Yesod and Tiphareth.

Direction: West (Above).

Astrological Correspondence:
    The zodiac sign of Sagittarius the Archer.

Description:
    This card is generally unvarying in design. From the very earliest Tarot decks, particularly the so-called Charles VI pack, the image of Temperance as a woman or angel pouring liquid from one container to another has been a constant, and it has always signified the mingling of opposites. In later decks, the central figure is undoubtedly an angel. Waite added iris flowers to represent the Greek meaning for the word iris, which is a rainbow. A smoldering volcano is shown in the background of his design. Crowley turned the central figure into a strange double-faced image representing alchemy, and he surrounded it by symbols of that mysterious art.

Symbolism:
    The angel of the card is usually identified with Gabriel, but sometimes with Michael. The important point of the card is the pouring from one bottle or cup into the other in a controlled flow. This mixing is further emphasized in some designs by the fact that the angel has one foot in the water and the other on solid ground. It has also been said that the angel personifies all the elements, standing on Water and Earth, with the wings representing Air while the halo (or the upwardly pointing triangle on the angel's chest) signifying Fire.
    The card is numbered 14, and this is the number of days in which the moon changes from full to new and new to full, so it is one half of the lunar cycle. Every symbol that is associated with

Temperance suggests transformation, and this is the reason that the card has been connected to the mystical medieval art of alchemy.

The golden cup represents the sphere of Tiphareth, which is ruled by the sun or the area of consciousness; the silver cup is Yesod, ruled by the moon, which is the region of the unconscious mind. The arc of the stream between them symbolizes the pathway between the two Sephirot. This stream resembles a rainbow connecting heaven and earth. In Norse mythology, the rainbow was seen as the Bifrost Bridge by which one could gain access to Asgard, the realm of the northern gods. Likewise in ancient Greek tradition, the rainbow was seen as a sign that the friendly messenger-goddess Iris was abroad. In fact, the word iris was used for both the rainbow and the flower of that name, both being symbolic of the goddess.

The astrological correspondence with Sagittarius might seem puzzling, since there is no image of a hunter included on the card. The curve of the rainbow may provide a clue, since it may be taken to resemble the arc of a hunter's bow. On the other hand, the usual image for Sagittarius is that of a centaur, who is half man and half horse. This is again a mingling of opposites that express the higher and lower natures.

In Qabalistic symbolism, the Hebrew letter associated with Temperance is Samekh, which means "the crutch, support or tent-peg." This refers to the nature of a safe haven and a shelter against the weather. A tent would blow away in a storm if it were not securely pegged to the ground. Safe within, the occupants can resist the tempest and await the rainbow that follows the downpour.

Upright Meaning:

This card symbolizes harmonious partnerships, the bringing together of things, and mixing and matching in order to achieve the best possible result. The basic message of Temperance is that moderation is the key to happiness, a message that is reflected to this day in a Greek saying: "Pan Metron Ariston" or "moderation in all things." If you have been pushing yourself or overdoing anything, then good sense and calm will soon prevail. The card also has a strongly spiritual side that suggests that contact with a universal force of love and compassion will become a feature of your existence. This is often accompanied by a feeling that there is someone on the "other side" who is looking out for you.

The angel of Temperance, numbered 14 in the major Arcana sequence, stands between the twin horrors of Death and the Devil. This is the calm between storms, careful manipulation of difficult circumstances and the cautious control of volatile forces.

If times have been difficult and you have suffered, possibly due to relationship break-up, the pain of bereavement, the anxiety of monetary hardship or some other distressing factor, then the arrival of Temperance in your reading is a very welcome omen. The card promises that your ills will be alleviated, your troubles ended and peace in your life will be restored. There is a need for the re-establishment of a tranquil normality after a period of knocks and setbacks, and this is exactly what the card indicates. Take heart, because you will soon learn to cope again, to smile, to forget worries and enjoy life once more. Temperance restores peace, not just your own peace of mind, but it will also dispel enmity and opposition. Disputes will be put to rest and warring parties will be brought to the negotiating table. Treaties and agreements of all kinds fall under the auspices of this most reasonable of cards.

Reversed Meaning:

Confrontation and opposition are indicated when the card is reversed. The lower nature dominates the higher, and unpleasant experiences are the result. You may be the victim of envy, with someone around you who sets out to undermine your confidence. The tension is such that quarrels are likely, especially in the home—although these will tend to be short lived. The reversed card may also indicate that certain people and places are not good for you and that they may even be very unfortunate. It also cautions against corrupt dealings that are opposed to your personal ethics.

XV (15)

The Devil

Alternative Titles: Temptation, Pan
Esoteric Titles: Lord of the Gates of Matter, Child of the
Forces of Time

Qabalistic Letter: Ayin, meaning eye. Number value 70.

Tree of Life Pathway: 16, from Hod to Tiphareth.

Direction: West (Below).

Astrological Correspondence:
The goat-like form of the Devil suggests a zodiacal connection to the sign of Capricorn.

Description:
The leering form of the Devil stands or crouches upon a square-cut plinth, his leathery wings outstretched. In many packs he holds a torch in his left hand while his right is raised in a mockery of blessing. The horns of the Devil sometimes appear to be attached to some form of headgear and they are reminiscent of the antlers of a stag or the branches of a tree. In other versions of the card, the horns of a ram or goat appear. In most designs, the head of the Devil forms an inverted pentagram, the symbol of depravity, black magic and of soul-less materialism. Two smaller demons stand tethered at his taloned feet, and both are usually horned like their master. Their hands are concealed behind their backs.

Symbolism:
At first glance this seems to be a conventional depiction of the Prince of Darkness, yet there are clues here which could indicate that a pagan fertility god such as the ancient Greek Pan, or the Celtic Horned One is the true subject of the card design. For example, the central Devil seems to be wearing a horned helmet rather than naturally possessing horns. This might indicate a shaman taking on the role of a nature god rather than the god himself.
Eliphas Levi was of the opinion that the card represented the alleged god of the Knights Templar, the mysterious Baphomet, and

illustrated his idea of Baphomet in a manner reminiscent of the Tarot Devil. However, medieval sources clearly state that Baphomet was represented as a severed human head, perhaps providing a link to ancient Celtic traditions (see the Four Grail Hallows) rather than being goat-like in nature. Another suggestion is that the card represents the bad guy of both the Persian Zoroastrian and Mithraist religions. The Templars have been suspected of being secret worshippers of the warrior sun god Mithras. Aleister Crowley suggested that the name Baphomet was a corruption of "Baphos Metr" which he translated as "Father Mithras." This may well be, but surely the Devil should represent not Mithras but his enemy Ahriman, the force of darkness and chaos, or his master Zervan, the grim god of cosmic time. It is interesting that both these were depicted winged, with bird's feet, as well as occasionally possessing horns. Zervan even bears a torch as one of his attributes.

The Romans had no difficulty in identifying the Persian Zervan with Saturn, their own gloomy god of time. This brings us full circle, because according to mythology, Saturn was bound and imprisoned in the underworld, much as the fallen angel Lucifer was. In addition, there is a similarity between the names Saturn and Satan. Satan is a word of Hebrew origin that literally means "the adversary," "the opponent" or putting it more bluntly, "the enemy." Thus Satan is a fitting title for an alter ego of Zervan/Saturn because the inexorable passage of time is the enemy of us all.

The two demons at the Devil's feet are obviously his prisoners, as we all are captives of time. They conceal their hands because they will take no action to either free themselves from their bonds or to improve their situation.

Finally, the cubic plinth upon which the Devil stands is symbolic of material reality, the four square certainties of life. Thus the Tarot Devil is revealed as the great tyrant and the harsh face of hard fact.

Upright Meaning:

It is vital to remember that this card signifies tyranny of one form or another. The obvious interpretation of the Devil card is one of temptation, of unfair obligation and being bound to some form of slavery. Its appearance may signal that you are not taking due note of the destructive consequences of your actions. The card may also show some immovable obstruction in your path. A direct confrontation will not work, because the Devil also represents overwhelming worldly power, so you will have to think laterally and to be cunning if you wish to overcome this difficulty.

When this card is present, it is worth questioning your motives; are you involved in anything ultimately negative, unworthy or spiteful? If so, the card gives you an opportunity to rectify the situation before time and events indicate that it is too late.

The Devil may also indicate greed and overly materialistic attitudes. Views (your own or those imposed upon you by another) that do not allow spiritual values or any independence of thought or action are indicated. The card can also point to the temptations of the flesh, to the kind of lust that grants you no peace, so it can indicate a passionate love affair based solely on sex. Addictions of all kinds fall within the Devil's realm. Pleasurable at first, but one easily becomes governed by the ultimately destructive habit.

Having said all that, it comes as a surprise to discover that the Devil is not always a bad card. By its nature it means permanence, admittedly usually of a negative sort, but when it comes to a committed partnership or marriage, the appearance of this card is a good sign showing that this link will stand the tests of time.

Reversed Meaning:

The bonds of the Devil are beginning to slacken when the card is reversed; just enough for you to remember what freedom is like. This provides the opportunity to ditch bad habits, addictions and destructive patterns of thought and behavior. You can now remove yourself from the company of those who have been negative influences.

XVI (16)

The Tower

Alternative Titles: The Tower of Destruction, The Falling Tower, The Tower of Babel, The Lightning-Struck Tower, The House of God, the Hospital, The Fire From Heaven, The Castle of Pluto, The Arrow, The Prison
Esoteric Title: Lord of the Hosts of the Mighty

Qabalistic Letter: Peh, meaning mouth. Number value 80.

Tree of Life Pathway: Twenty-seventh, between Hod and Netzah.

Direction: North.

Astrological Correspondence:
Mars, the bringer of war.

Description:
Although this card may be titled in many different ways, the actual image of the Tower rarely varies from deck to deck. A strongly built, lofty tower, with three narrow windows set high in its wall is perched on the crest of a hill. A bolt of lightning (often resembling an arrow) descends from the heavens, striking the tower and causing enormous damage. The very top of the structure, resembling castle battlements or a crown, is dislodged while the interior of the building becomes a raging inferno, the flames and sparks of which can be seen issuing from the broken roof and the windows of the fortress. Two figures tumble headfirst from a great height; either they have been blown out by the force of the blast or have hurled themselves from the tower in a desperate attempt to escape the flames.

Symbolism:
The fall of the Tower is a potent image, which at various times has been linked to God's punishment of the cities of Sodom and Gomorrah, the destruction of the island empire of Atlantis and the burning of the Temple of Jerusalem. Some have seen it as the collapse of the power structure of the Roman Catholic Church that was so ardently desired by many groups of medieval heretics. In each of these cases, perceived corruption is punished by an act of God that is swift and terrible. On the other hand, it is likely that the Tower of the card actually represents the Biblical tale of the Tower of Babel found in the Book of Genesis. This lofty structure was

built at the command of King Nimrod, the "mighty hunter," a descendant of Noah. Nimrod, insane with pride, wanted a tower that was so high that by scaling it he could invade heaven itself to take revenge on God and his angels because they had drowned so many of his ancestors in the Great Flood. However, before the vast building was completed, God smote Nimrod and his servants with a "confusion of tongues" and since that day, mankind has spoken many languages, making mutual understanding and co-operation between the peoples of the world difficult.

The Hebrew letter Peh, meaning mouth, is associated with this card. This is apt because the mouth is the source of speech, the primary organ of communication. It should also be remembered that the card is astrologically connected to the aggressive influence of the planet Mars, the "Lord of the Hosts of the Mighty" of the card's esoteric title. Taking this into account Peh, the mouth, may also stand for a war cry or a challenge to combat.

Mars is first and foremost a masculine planet, forceful, assertive and dominant. The red planet influences the physical desires and the sex drive. It has been pointed out that the explosive image of the Tower is reminiscent of an ejaculating phallus. This is another potent and apt symbol for this martial card.

The thunderbolt itself is the primary attribute of deities such as Zeus/Jupiter and the Norse Thor and it was a weapon in their wars against the forces of chaos. In Buddhist symbolism the lightning flash is a masculine force representing a sudden awakening of realization to inescapable truth. The Roman writer Plutarch said that lightning gave fertility to the ground it struck.

Upright Meaning:

As might be imagined from the violent image of the card, the appearance of the Tower forecasts a lot of turmoil and disruption. However, there is a positive side to this card, even though it is hard to find. A major positive aspect that is hidden is the concept of gaining freedom, albeit after your sense of personal security is seriously threatened. It could be that a whole value system has reached the point of collapse and this harsh fact will force a reassessment of one's life. Deeply held beliefs and rock-solid certainties will not seem as reliable as they once did. It is possible that this reassessment of your life, your position and your beliefs will be forced upon you by some personal upset or even as the result of a tragedy. Comfortable illusions are shattered, which will be a painful process, yet the newly perceived reality that emerges from the wreckage of the past will open your eyes to the truth.

The terrible shock that this card indicates will not last forever. You will come out of this experience a stronger, wiser and more capable person. To paraphrase the German philosopher Friedrich Nietzsche, "What does not destroy you, makes you stronger" and this is the case with this violent card. The Tower card opens doorways that you would never open by your own volition. In some ways, it removes options in the short term, but opens up so many new possibilities that you could not imagine their scope when the time comes for you to start to look a little further forward along life's pathway.

After the fierce lightning blast you could be left feeling dazed and bewildered. Now you will need a breathing space to think and time to plan your next course of action. The point is that you are now free of all those things that once held you back. You may be starting again from square one, but now you will be better prepared, and free to make your own decisions in the sure knowledge that you will not repeat your past mistakes.

Reversed Meaning:

You may be falsely accused of something, or you could feel isolated, oppressed or even experience some form of imprisonment. You could be rebelling against tyranny, showing a side to your character that is a shock to those around you. It may even be you who provides the lightning bolt that overthrows any oppressive conditions that afflict you. Whether this rebellion is a good or a bad thing will be revealed by the rest of your reading.

XVII (17)

The Star

Alternative Title: The Stars
*Esoteric Titles: Daughter of the Firmament, Dweller
between Waters*

Qabalistic Letter: This pathway is associated with the Hebrew letter Tzaddi, meaning the fish hook. According to Mathers and the Golden Dawn, this pathway belongs to the Star, however Aleister Crowley seemingly arbitrarily altered the sequence by allocating the Star to the letter He, usually ascribed to the Emperor. The number value of Tzaddi is 90, while He's number value is 5.

Tree of Life Pathway: 18, from Yesod to Netzah, or path 5 between Tiphareth and Hokmah, according to Crowley.

Direction: South (above).

Astrological Correspondence:
The Star is fairly obviously associated with the sign of Aquarius the Water Carrier.

Description:
The image of a young girl pouring water from two vessels upon the earth and into a pool. She kneels beneath a sky spangled with eight stars, one of which is larger and brighter than the rest. Often, a bird, usually taken to be a dove, but occasionally identified as an eagle or an ibis, perches in a tree in the background. This is a design that rarely varies from one Tarot deck to another. However some variations do occasionally occur, such as in the fifteenth century design attributed to Antonio di Cicognara that shows a crowned queen with a star in her upraised right hand or as a conventional nativity scene with the three Magi and the Star of Bethlehem.

Symbolism:
The great central star that gives the card its name can be identified with either Venus, the so-called Morning Star or with Sirius, the brightest star in the heavens. The connection with Venus (or Aphrodite) is striking, since this goddess was reputed to appear

as a naked nymph. A dove symbolizes her and she was indeed born from water. Venus was also considered to be a goddess of nature, so she could be thought of as pouring out the waters of new life to restore the fertility of the earth in the springtime.

Another view suggests that the star is Sirius the "dog star." This, the brightest of stars, was associated with the ancient Egyptian mother-goddess Isis. After a seventy-day period (the seven lesser stars?) during which the star was invisible, Sirius would rise again around the time of the Summer solstice. The day upon which Sirius rose signaled the annual inundation of the Nile, beginning the Egyptian New Year and the promise of prosperity, good harvests and plenty for the following twelve months. The occasion was celebrated at the Opet festival, a joyous celebration of fertility and life. In this case, the ibis bird would be an apt symbol for the card, because in Egyptian belief the ibis was symbolic of Thoth, the god of wisdom and regulator of time. In addition, the beak of the ibis is a perfect fishhook, as in the Qabalistic symbolism of the card.

Some have identified the central figure as Ganymede; however, according to Greek mythology, Ganymede was a handsome Trojan Prince who was carried off by Zeus (Jupiter) in the form of an eagle, to become the cupbearer to the gods of Olympus. This is a far cry from the beautiful girl of the Tarot design. There may be a vague connection, because Ganymede was said to have become the zodiac sign of Aquarius. The star-pattern that makes up the constellation of Aquila the Eagle is in the same quadrant of the sky.

Upright Meaning:

The Star has a positive message to give. This is an uplifting card; it is extremely optimistic in nature, bringing hope, a renewal of faith and gifts. The appearance of the Star indicates that problems will be solved, life will become easier and you will feel far more healthy and lively. A positive, optimistic frame of mind is to be expected and indeed your prospects will improve. This is a card of luck. New opportunities, a renewed sense of security and a far more promising set of circumstances await you.

The Star is an indicator of good health and may indicate the improvement of a medical condition. Equally likely is that educational or artistic matters are indicated. If so, then success in your endeavors is shown. Vacations are in tune with the optimism of this card, so traveling for fun is indicated, or just that the Star foretells an expansive, happy-go-lucky, carefree feeling.

The Star is also associated with spirituality. An underlying theme is that of awakening to the fact that life has a pattern and a meaning.

It would be wise to note in which area of your reading the Star occurs, because its message of hope will apply to that sphere of life. If, for instance, it should appear in a position that refers to career, then it is likely that a new, more fulfilling job is imminent. If it should appear in the area of romance, then love will blossom in your life.

Reversed Meaning:

Although the Star is still a positive card, the outlook may be tense when it is reversed or surrounded by cards of darker meaning. There may be a lack of self-belief apparent, even though the prospects remain good. You may feel that you have been disappointed so many times in the past that you refuse to hope any more and that you have become a pessimist and a cynic. Your once-bright hopes may have been dashed, yet you will soon be surprised by a stroke of good luck. If opportunities seem thin on the ground, be patient, because the right doorway will open to you very soon—whether you believe it or not!

Some people take this card as an indication that the questioner should or will take up the study of astrology.

XVIII (18)

The Moon

Alternative Title: Illusion
Esoteric Titles: Ruler of Flux and Reflux, Child of the
Sons of the Mighty

Qabalistic Letter: Qoph, meaning back of the head. Number value 100.

Tree of Life Pathway: Nineteenth, between Malkuth and Netzah.

Direction: South (below).

Astrological Correspondence:
Surprisingly, the Moon card does not correlate to the moon of astrology, neither does it symbolize the moon's own sign of Cancer the Crab, despite having a lobster or crawfish included in the design. Instead, both the Golden Dawn and Crowley ascribe the card to the sign of Pisces and its symbol, the two fish.

Description:
In most versions of this card, a pale moon sheds drops of dew or blood while shining wanly down onto a desolate landscape. Two ominous towers frame the scene, while a dog and a wolf howl mournfully. A narrow, twisting path wends its way to the horizon, while from a deep pool in the foreground of this forbidding spectacle a lobster or crayfish painfully crawls up onto the land.

Apparently in an effort to make the card's sinister imagery more palatable, several designers sought to reinterpret the Moon and render the card less ominous. In one early nineteenth century version, the moon is veiled by clouds, the towers have become lighthouses and two greyhounds gambol around a lobster on a dish. In another card design, a young man playing a lute serenades his lover, who gazes down at him from her balcony. Aleister Crowley chose to reinvent the traditional image in ancient Egyptian terms. The dogs become depictions of jackal-headed Anubis, the god of embalming, while the crayfish is transformed into Khepera, the scarab beetle that was the creator-god of the dawn.

Symbolism:

The nineteenth pathway is that of the Moon, leading from Malkuth to Netzah, the sphere of passions. The Moon card is related to the letter Qoph meaning "Back of Head," referring to the primitive brain and the controller of autonomic functions that keep the body running at all times, even when asleep. This is apt, because this card is indicative of dreams, and as we shall see, also nightmares.

The Qabalistic pathway symbolized by the Moon card requires courage, for it takes us through the dark and perilous realms of the subconscious mind to find the hidden drives that control our attitudes and our actions. In this sinister region may be found our own personal demons, those horrors that lurk in the dark corners of our minds in the form of phobias and neuroses. These challenges are symbolized in the card as a dog and a wolf howling at the moon above, and by the dark pool from which crawls the primeval form of the crayfish.

Astrologically ruled by Pisces, the two fish who are denizens of the darkest depths, this pathway shows us illusions and deceptions. It also reveals the power of the imagination and the ability to give our inner desires concrete form. The winding path leading to the horizon in the card's design also suggests the symbolism of Pisces. A path makes contact with the feet, and that is the bodily area associated with this watery sign of the zodiac.

In his "Book of Thoth," Aleister Crowley wrote, "This is the waning moon, the moon of witchcraft and abominable deeds. She is the poisoned darkness which is the condition of the rebirth of light."

Upright Meaning:

When the pale Moon appears in a reading, you can be absolutely sure that nothing is what it seems to be! It is very likely that some extremely highly charged emotions are causing complete havoc in someone's life. Everything seems to be viewed through the filter of unruly feelings. There is hidden meaning in everything and paranoia is rife. There is a need to step back, regain some perspective and take a look at your anxieties with a cool, dispassionate attitude. This is easier said than done, because this form of emotional detachment is never going to be easy. Having said that, it is true that the path you seem to be on is an extremely difficult one, yet it is the right one for you, with all its twists and turns and its snares for the unwary. So, you need to keep right on to the end of the road and to continue along your course even when you feel that carrying on is a hopeless activity. All will turn out all right in the end. The weak light of the moon may be deceptive, but it does actually show the way, even if you do sometimes lose sight of the long-term goal.

On a more positive note, the illusion signified by this card can be used to good effect. Your imagination will be stimulated and you might find yourself inspired to express yourself in a creative manner. Even the most troublesome emotional turmoil can inspire a work of genius.

If by any chance you might be involved in a clandestine love affair, the appearance of the Moon is said to be favorable for this secret activity.

Reversed Meaning:

The reversed Moon is a warning that you are being intentionally misled. The anxieties shown by the upright card may be illusions, yet when the card is reversed they have a factual basis. There is cause for concern because there are enemies and traps around, and you will need to take great care to avoid the pitfalls. Lies and insincerity are likely to be features of your life at the moment. Do not allow yourself to be fooled, no matter how much you want to believe in glittering falsehoods. Needless to say, the Moon in this position is not good for those involved in clandestine love affairs, and it is likely that the truth will emerge!

Despite the traditional interpretation that I have given above, I have noticed time and again that the Moon card is not a good one where relationship matters are concerned. When someone is looking for commitment in a relationship, and the Moon card turns up, in either upright or reversed position, the relationship does not work out in the end. If the question concerns a business or financial matter, the subject is being deceived or mistreated.

XIX (19)

The Sun

Esoteric Title: Lord of the Fire of the World

Qabalistic Letter: Resh, meaning head of the body. Number value 200.

Tree of Life Pathway: Twentieth, between Yesod and Hod.

Direction: South.

Astrological Correspondence:

For once there is no mistaking the astrological attribution, because the Tarot Sun corresponds exactly to the astrological sun.

Description:

A glorious, beaming sun shines his benevolence down into a walled garden in this happy card; the smiling solar disk is surrounded by both straight and wavering rays. Water droplets seem to fall from the sun in some versions, while in others they are drawn upwards in a process of evaporation. In one of the earliest Tarot decks (the so-called Charles VI pack), a young woman spins yarn in the sun's light, but in most old versions, children are featured as the occupants of the walled garden. The fifteenth century "Bembo" deck shows the sun's disc in the upraised hand of a laughing child. In more conventional variants, such as the Marseilles Tarot, two children playfully embrace beneath the smiling solar disk. Even Crowley is content to follow this tradition while including the twelve signs of the zodiac within the sun's beams. Waite's deck shows a smiling child riding a white horse while holding a large banner. Behind the horse and his diminutive rider, the wall of the garden is crowned with four sunflowers.

Symbolism:

The pathway is associated with the Sun card and leads from Yesod to Hod, the sphere of wisdom. Here the bright rays pierce all confusion and lead to awareness. The twentieth pathway is the road of truth on which all deceptions are banished. Of course this searing light may also destroy cherished illusions, stripping bare the soul and revealing basic motivations, but it also emphasizes such concepts as individuality. Here, a consciousness of oneself as an integral and self-regenerating part of the life-force may be experienced.

The Hebrew letter for this pathway is Resh, meaning "Head," which is taken to be the higher faculties of consciousness. It may also suggest the higher self, the Holy Guardian Angel, the part of us that knows better than our small, selfish, limited egos. Resh can also be taken as the start of something—perhaps a new month or a New Year, sometimes even the top of the page or the start of a project.

The twin children that are often found dancing at the foot of the card can be suggestive of the sign of Gemini, but this sign has little to do with either the symbolism of the card or the pathway—other than it serves to represent the concept of duality. The glorious sun above is both a protective and a threatening force, as it sheds droplets of light to guide the divided soul to the infinity of solar oneness.

In Waite's version of the card, a child is mounted on a white horse. This child expresses the words of Jesus, "Except ye become as little children, ye shall not enter into the kingdom of heaven." Therefore, this child (or the two children) could represent the soul, while the horse would stand for the physical body.

The four sunflowers seen on some versions of the card may stand for the four elements and for the four Jungian "functions" of sensation, feeling, thinking and intuition.

Upright Meaning:

You do not need to know much about the Tarot to realize that the smiling Sun is considered to be one of the best cards in the entire Tarot deck. The sunny mood of the image is buoyant and uplifting, and its appearance indicates good health, happiness, romance and emotional fulfillment, children and joyous times.

There may be excellent news concerning children or perhaps the birth of a child. You may have a reunion with old and cherished friends as well as enjoyable times spent with agreeable companions and days that are filled with laughter.

The Sun shows that difficulties will be overcome and this situation is often accompanied by at least some degree of fame, or at the very least a recognition of your achievements. The Sun card does not actually offer wealth, though it does seem to indicate the right conditions conducive to obtaining prosperity.

One important feature of this card should not be overlooked, which is that it is said to brighten all the other cards in a reading; so even if the other cards are filled with doom and gloom, the appearance of the Sun at least promises a happy ending. This is particularly true when considering health issues, as it signifies that troublesome ailments will soon be gone, and your general state of health will improve.

The Sun can also be used as an indication of timing during a reading. It can signify the summer season—possibly that you will spend time in a hot, sunny place, or at the very least you will be basking in the warmth of popularity.

Reversed Meaning:

The Sun can never be a bad card, even when reversed. There may well be some delays, but the essentially joyous message of the card remains the same, upright or reversed. Good news is still on its way and you are going to be pleasantly surprised. All that you need to do is to keep your feet on the ground and not allow your good fortune to go to your head. The only possible negative interpretation of this card is that it may show a tendency to become arrogant. Even so, you are still likely to be in the right, even if you do appear to be rather immodest.

XX (20)

Judgement

Alternative Titles: The Angel, The Last Trump, The Eon,
Awakening
Esoteric Title: Spirit of the Primal Fire

Qabalistic Letter: Shin, meaning tooth. Number value 300.

Tree of Life Pathway: 21, from Malkuth to Hod.

Direction: North to South.

Astrological Correspondence:

The Element of Fire according to Mathers and Crowley. More modern commentators have attributed the Judgement card to the planet Pluto.

Description:

In most traditional Tarot decks the image on the card of Judgement is a conventional Christian scene from the Apocalypse of St. John. A fiery angel sounds the last trump; graveyards yawn and give up their dead, who stand with arms upraised at the moment of their resurrection. However, in some packs of the Renaissance period, the figure of the angel is replaced by that of God himself. In total contrast, in Aleister Crowley's own version of the Tarot, the card is replaced by one called "The Aeon," in which the child-like form of the Egyptian god Horus waits to usher in a new era in the history of the world. This new epoch, according to Crowley was to be called the Age of Horus, its dominant religion was to be the faith of "Do what thou wilt" as interpreted by Crowley himself.

Symbolism:

The pathway of Judgement joins the earthly sphere of Malkuth, governed by the planet Saturn, to Hod the sphere of wisdom associated with the planet Mercury. The card itself is symbolically connected to the element of Fire, and in recent years, to the planet Pluto.

In his Qabalistic writings, A.E Waite was prompted to ask, "What is it that within us sounds a trumpet?" The answer to that question seems to be "desire," as symbolized by the flames of passion of the fiery element. It could also be a yearning for answers in general, which can only be fulfilled by a mental journey to the sphere of wisdom itself. Indeed the angel who sounds the "Last Trump" is not Gabriel (associated with the Water element) as commonly thought but the fiery archangel Michael. This archangel has been traditionally considered to be the governing spirit of the planet Mercury and is a "Christianization" of the Roman god of that name.

Mercury (and his Greek predecessor Hermes) was worshipped as the messenger of the gods but he did have another role, that of guide to the dead and thus conveying the souls of the departed to the mysterious realm of Pluto. Pluto was the ancient Roman god of death, so this is another pathway that hints at the soul achieving freedom at the demise of the physical body.

In terms of astrology, the far distant planet Pluto is considered to be the orb of transformation. Its influence brings profound changes in life and it is associated with fundamental meaning and the harsh workings of fate. Yet, Pluto is a necessary influence indicating the time for a change. It is associated with evolution, not just of the individual but also of the masses.

The Hebrew letter Shin represents the twenty-first pathway. Its alternative meaning, "tooth" suggests both biting through obstacles and the discomfort of teething. At the risk of being flippant, the pathway of Judgement gives us plenty to chew on.

Upright Meaning:

The fanfare of the Last Trump sounds, and its mighty blast, its clarion call, cannot be ignored. It signals both an ending and a new beginning. This is certainly the end of one phase of life, but this is not a cause for regret. Let the past go, for there are bigger, better, more worthwhile things to come. It is likely that new opportunities are about to present themselves when this card appears. Each of these will have far-reaching implications because they are bound to change your life and your opinions in dramatic ways. Nevertheless, before you move on you will have the chance to look back and to assess your accomplishments. After all, this is the card of logical conclusion, an end of an era. You can now face the future with a clear conscience and the knowledge that you have done well. You will rightly feel that you have done your duty and performed to the best of your ability. This knowledge grants a new lease of life and the confidence to take on a more challenging role. The card also shows that you will now have the opportunity to do all those things that you have put on hold simply because you were so busy. In addition, the appearance of the Judgement card is traditionally held to speed up the pace of events, so that whatever is predicted in your Tarot reading will occur more quickly than is otherwise indicated. Another traditional meaning associated with this card relates to legal disputes. The upright Judgement card shows that legal rulings will be in your favor.

Reversed Meaning:

Annoying delays are shown when Judgement is reversed. You may be providing a few of these delays yourself because you are afraid of the far-reaching implications of dramatic change in your life. You may wish to avoid responsibility or to ignore the new opportunities. However, like it or not, change is on the way! There may be an over-reliance on habit and routine. In short, the reversed Judgement could indicate a denial of the inevitable. It may also show that a fear of illness and death may prevent someone from seeking necessary medical treatment. When this card is reversed, it serves to slow down events and also indicates legal problems with rulings going against you.

XXI (21)

The World

Alternative Title: The Universe
Esoteric Title: Great One of the Night of Time

Qabalistic Letter: Tau, meaning cross. Number value 400.

Tree of Life Pathway: Twenty-second, from Yesod to Malkuth.

Direction: Center.

Astrological Correspondence:
    The World card is associated with the planet Saturn.

Description:
    In most Tarot decks, the image of the World card is a purely symbolic one. Within a wreath of victory, a naked maiden dances and a light veil that is wrapped about her body preserves her modesty. She is often shown balancing on a small globe or floating in space itself. In her hands she holds two small wands. The four corners of the card are occupied by the "four holy living creatures" spoken of by the Biblical prophet Ezekiel. These are the lion, the bull, the man and the eagle.

Symbolism:
    According to Mathers and Crowley, this card is associated with the twenty-second pathway, which leads from the material world of Malkuth to Yesod, the sphere of the Moon. In the Golden Dawn symbolism, The World is connected to the harsh, restrictive planet Saturn, while the dancing maiden of the card is indicative of freedom and joy. This apparent contradiction is explained as the death of the body releasing the soul. This makes even more sense when we consider that Saturn also represents old age.
    The Hebrew letter Tau, meaning "cross," also symbolizes this pathway. The cross symbol is suggestive of material reality in more ways than one. It can represent the four directions, the four seasons and the four classical elements of Earth, Air, Fire and Water. In the World card, four symbolic beasts are positioned at the corners of the card (these four have already appeared in the Major Arcana in The Chariot and The Wheel).

In medieval art, these figures are often used to represent the four elements of astrology—Fire, Earth, Air and Water as well as the "fixed" signs of the zodiac associated with them. These are Leo the lion, Taurus the bull, Aquarius the water carrier and finally, Scorpio, here shown in its more spiritual form as an eagle rather than the more familiar scorpion. However they can also symbolize the four seasons—summer, spring, winter and fall, as well as the four "corners of the earth" or cardinal directions, which are South, East, North and West.

To give a more conventionally Christian spin to these creatures, they also became associated with—and symbolic of—the Four Disciples. So, we also have the lion of St. Mark, the bull of St. Luke, the human symbol of St. John and the eagle of St. Matthew, each likewise connected with a direction, element, season and sign of the zodiac. Such is the nature of symbolism that the four beasts appear simultaneously in all these roles within the card.

The identity of the central dancing figure is more problematic. Most commentators believe that this is a female who may represent "mother nature." However, some have expressed doubts on this point, suggesting that the dancer possesses both genders and is the "divine androgyne" symbolizing the unification of opposites. If the views of the heretical Gnostic Christians are taken into account, then this may be a depiction of the Aeon—the "anima mundi," the soul of the world, who was seen as an intermediary between the individual spirit and the universal. Their use of the very word Aeon brings us to its modern derivative "Eon," so the dancing figure may therefore be seen as a symbol of cosmic time.

Upright Meaning:

By common consent this card is thought of as one of the best to find in a reading. Its appearance signals that the longed-for reward, the success, the triumph promised by so many of the other cards is now imminent. The World usually means that happiness and feelings of justifiable pride will soon follow. This is an indication that you will achieve your heart's desire, whatever that desire might be!

There is no doubt that you will have experienced many trials and difficulties but those who have witnessed them will appreciate all the struggles you have endured. Good friends will now applaud your triumph and grant you the respect and admiration that you deserve. You have reached the end of an era: the cycle is complete, the final transformation is here and you can now bask in the knowledge that you have done your best and won against the odds.

If your question is about love, then you can be sure that a perfect, fulfilling relationship will soon be yours. For some people, the card will mean fame, extensive influence and worldly power, for others it can signal wealth that can be material or of the spiritual variety. The World shows that your dearest dream and most cherished ambition will come to pass.

As if victory and happy achievements were not enough, The World can also provide a signal to go out into the world, to travel and enjoy the fruits of your labors. So, a much-needed vacation is often indicated by the appearance of this card.

Reversed Meaning:

Even when reversed, this card is never really negative. It may show that you still have a little way to go before you achieve your dreams. It suggests that you should not lose heart or decide to change direction, because you are about to make a significant breakthrough. On the other hand, an old ambition that is now within your grasp may not have the same appeal as it once did. Another possibility is that you may be nervous about finally achieving your goal and a little afraid of success and all its implications. It may be that you feel envious of someone else's success, when you are perfectly capable of achieving the same triumph for yourself but seem to be unwilling to make the effort.

16

Reading the Cards

Tarot cards can be read in a variety of ways. Most people use the full deck of 78 cards, while others prefer to use only the 22 cards of the Major Arcana. Of course, those who read ordinary playing cards are effectively reading the Minor Arcana, although the interpretations for each playing card don't necessarily match up with those used by Tarot card readers. It is also acceptable to start with an initial reading using the Major cards to focus on important issues, following up with a reading using the full deck to highlight details. In fact, this is a very traditional way of reading cards, as will be shown later in this chapter.

The Significator

Many Tarot readers choose a card to represent the person for whom they are reading. Some even select a card to represent the question that they are asking. The Lovers is often used for affairs of the heart, the Ace of Coins for finances or the Chariot, the Eight of Wands or Cups or the Six of Swords for embarking on a journey. Such a card is called a Significator. In most cases, the Significator will be one of the court cards of the Minor Arcana, based upon the appearance, character, profession or star sign of the questioner. However, it is traditionally acceptable to use the Magician for a man or the Priestess for a woman if you cannot make up your mind which King, Queen, Knight or Page is most apt.

Beginning the Reading

It is essential to be in a passive state of mind for meaningful card divination. A few deep breaths will help you to relax as you shuffle and divide the Tarot deck. Allow yourself to drift into a calm and peaceful mental state. Those who use reversed cards as part of their reading should turn some during the shuffle. If you are reading for someone else, you should then hand the deck to the inquirer, who should repeat the process of mixing the cards up thoroughly. When the cards are returned, you should lay out a number of them in an appropriate arrangement called a spread.

Laying Out the Cards

Before we tackle individual Tarot spreads, we should remember that the cards, like many other divination tools, will tend to focus on drama and large events that make an emotional impact. This drama may have already happened, be occurring now or it may still be a way off in the future—although the first spread usually focuses on fairly immediate matters. Therefore, if an apparently dreadful card such as the Ten of Swords or the Devil appears, it does not necessarily predict horrors to come; it might just as easily provide a background to upcoming events.

When beginning to read the cards, it is not always a good idea to look immediately to the future. Begin by mentally asking the cards to link you to the present situation. Then tell your inquirer about the things that are happening to him now. If you find this initial part of the reading accurate, then the rest of it will also be accurate.

Try not to develop any preconceptions before beginning the reading. The future is a tricky thing and the cards can actually deceive you by telling you the absolute truth. It is all in how you interpret them. If you have any fixed ideas about what is to come and you then go on to shape your reading according to these preconceptions, you are likely to mislead yourself.

The Art of Reading the Cards

As with any practice of divination, card reading brings great responsibilities. People will take what you say very seriously indeed, even if they appear to be flippant or skeptical. It is not your place to upset or frighten people who actually need a little guidance along life's road. It is worse when the cards are bad, so a great deal of care needs to be taken when breaking disturbing news. In my view, it is best to be discrete—so when you are in doubt about what to say or how to say it, then it is best to consider the inquirer's peace of mind and remain silent.

Tarot Spreads

There are many traditional Tarot spreads and most books on card reading will present a selection of them. In this book, I thought it would be a good idea to show some spreads that have an astrological or Qabalistic basis, and some that are just generally very useful. These are explained in the following pages.

The Horoscope Spread

This spread of thirteen cards can be used in two ways. It is a general pattern that does not require a specific question, so it can reflect the twelve houses of the horoscope, each of which reflect a different sphere of life. It can also be used to give a forecast for the whole year, month by month.

Card	Zodiac Sign	Area of Influence
1	Aries	The personality and outward expression of the inquirer.
2	Taurus	Money, possessions and material affairs.
3	Gemini	Learning, short journeys, communication and siblings.
4	Cancer	Home life, heritage, origins and childhood.
5	Leo	Romance, creativity, fun, offspring.
6	Virgo	Work, habits, health.
7	Libra	Long-term relationships, both personal and professional.
8	Scorpio	Sexuality, investments, inheritance and shared resources.
9	Sagittarius	Distant travel, beliefs and higher learning.
10	Capricorn	Career, status and ambitions.
11	Aquarius	Friendships, social life, hopes, aspirations and desires.
12	Pisces	Secrets, psychological pressures, hidden enemies, or becoming one's own worst enemy.
Central Card		An overview, a general indicator of fortune.

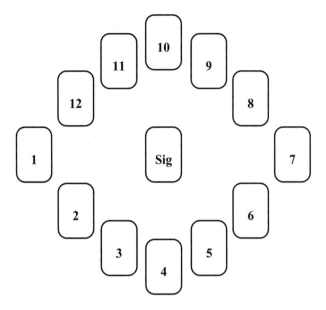

If further details are required or if you wish to give extra clarification to any point in the reading, it is permissible to place two cards in the relevant positions in order to gain extra information.

An interesting aspect of this spread is that each card already has its astrological significance, so the interplay between this and the card's position in a reading will add another dimension to the interpretation.

The Planetary Spread

This spread can be used to answer a specific question or to give a weekly forecast.

First select a significator to occupy the central position, and then shuffle the cards.

Lay the top seven cards down in the following pattern.

Card	The Planet and its Position
1	The position of the Moon relating to domestic and family issues.
2	The position of Mercury relating to business, skill and communications.
3	The position of Venus relating to affairs of the heart and the emotions in general.
4	The position of the Sun relating to achievements and the sense of self.
5	The position of Mars relating to opposition, aggression and self-assertion.
6	The position of Jupiter relating to money, gain, wealth and profits.
7	The position of Saturn relating to restrictions, duties, problems and obstacles.

If a contradiction appears to occur between various cards, then the resolution to this conflict will be found in position two—that of Mercury, the mediator.

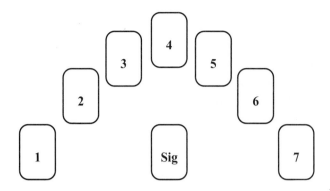

This spread can also be used as a weekly forecast, simply because each of the seven classical planets traditionally governs a day of the week.

Card	Planet	Day
1	Moon	Monday
2	Mercury	Wednesday
3	Venus	Friday
4	Sun	Sunday
5	Mars	Tuesday
6	Jupiter	Thursday
7	Saturn	Saturday

The Tree of Life Spread—One

The pattern of the Qabalistic Tree of Life is an obvious basis for a Tarot spread. This pattern can be used in two distinct ways. The first is reasonably straightforward, as one simply shuffles and mixes the cards and then arranges ten to correspond to the positions of the Sephirot from Kether (number 1) to Malkuth (number 10). Fur further information on the Sephirot, see the chapter on The Holy Qabalah.

Card	Sephira	Meaning
1	Kether	Spiritual matters.
2	Hokmah	Initiate and responsibilities.
3	Binah	Limitations and sorrows.
4	Hesed	Factors that are constructive and also financial affairs.
5	Geburah	Factors that are destructive or that oppose you.
6	Tiphareth	Reputation and achievements.
7	Netzah	Love and relationships that are personal or professional.
8	Hod	Communication, business and intelligence.
9	Yesod	Health, dreams and the workings of the unconscious mind.
10	Malkuth	Home and family.

The Tree of Life Spread—Two

The second way of using the Tree of Life pattern is a little more complicated but often more revealing than the first. Begin by choosing a significator, make a note of which card you have chosen and put it back into the pack. If this is a personal reading, choose a card that is representative of the person for whom you are reading. If on the other hand, an issue is prominent in the inquirer's mind; choose a card that is symbolic of the question.

Shuffle the cards thoroughly and then deal out the full pack in the Tree of Life pattern from 1 to 10, then from 1 to 10 again until you have no cards left. Taking each pile in turn, find the one that

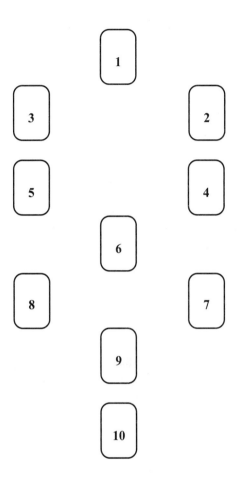

contains the significator. This will show the area of special interest. All that remains is to read the cards within that pile, relating them to the themes of the Sephira that they represent. This may appear to be a long winded way of finding a few cards, but the process of laying the cards out becomes a form of meditation or "intunement" that takes you and your inquirer away from everyday life and encourages you to open up any intuitive or psychic gifts that you may have.

The Pyramid Spread

Over the past 150 years, many people have tried to link the Tarot to ancient Egypt, but as we have discovered, any such connection is tenuous and it only comes down to us through the Hebrew connection via the Qabalah. However, for those who feel spiritually attached to the idea of Egypt and the power of the pyramid shape, here is a suitable spread.

Ask your inquirer to shuffle the cards well and then take them from him. Lay the cards out face downwards in the pyramid shape shown, left to right, starting with the four cards at the base and then working upwards. Then turn over the cards one row at a time, again working upwards from the base.

The four cards at the base of the pyramid refer to the inquirer's current situation.

The three-card row shows how this will develop.

The two-card row indicates the outcome of the present situation.

The top card may refer to the ultimate outcome of the present set of circumstances, or it may point towards the start of a completely different one that has yet to arise.

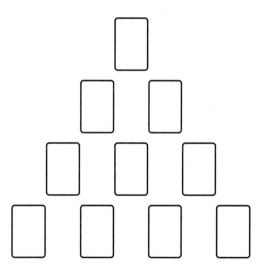

Answering Questions

All Tarot readers know that the best way of getting the intuitive juices flowing is to give a reading to another person, and we all know how difficult it is to give ourselves a reading. There is no harm in reading for ourselves, but we are usually so close to our own problems that it is hard to be subjective, and we bring our own hopes, fears and impressions to the reading.

Having said this, there are times when we need to make a quick decision or to get a straight answer to a question. The following two spreads will help us to do just that. Neither of these spreads is solely for self-use; you can always use either or both of them to answer a question for someone else. These spreads are especially useful when a friend telephones you or drops in and asks you for a quick bit of guidance. Remember to look at the Qabalistic and astrological significances so that you can see everything that relates to the question and the answer that the cards give you.

The Past, Present and Future Spread

Shuffle the cards and focus your mind on the question.

Then, lay out two cards to represent the past, two for the present and two more for the future.

The cards that symbolize the past will show you the root of the current problem, the ones that denote the present will show you how this is developing at present and the last two will suggest how the situation will be resolved (or otherwise) in the future.

Remember that, if a Major Arcana turns up anywhere in the spread, there is an element of fate that is taking a hand.

Past   **Present**   **Future**

When You Need a Quick Answer

Shuffle the cards while concentrating on your question.

Select four cards at random from the deck and place them face downwards on the table.

Choose one card from the four and let that stand as a significator of the question.

Now turn over each of the remaining three cards and see what answers they give you. If you have more than one possible path that you could take, then you can repeat this layout, with each reading representing one possible choice of action.

Remember to consider the Qabalistic and astrological significance to your answer, as that will add information to the basic Tarot interpretation.

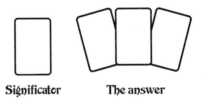

Significator   The answer

The Pathways Spread

Here is another way of choosing between two paths of action:

Shuffle the cards and concentrate on your question.
Now lay out three cards to represent the likely outcome to one choice of action and another three for the alternative choice of action.

Add to your interpretation of the cards by checking to see if they suggest a particular season of the year or a direction, as this may show you when and where the answer to your problem lies.

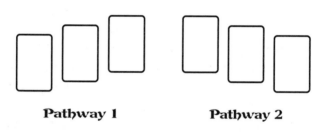

Pathway 1   **Pathway 2**

Conclusion

No matter how much we know about the Tarot, it is not the whole story. People read the cards in their own way, and this is only right and proper. Unlike the Ten Commandments, the interpretations for the Tarot are not set in stone. Tarot has existed for hundreds of years and over time it has evolved—and all things being equal, it will continue to do so. It is not for yesterday or today alone; indeed it is for all the tomorrows that have yet to come.

We should not forget the wisdom and ingenuity of those who have gone before us—rather, while knowing and understanding the thinking behind these earlier interpretations, we should go forward and apply our own common sense, experience and intuition to the vexed questions that will come our way in the present and the future.

It must by now be obvious to you that I love to explore history, mythology and the deliberations of the mystics and thinkers who have gone before me, and researching this book has taken me down some fascinating roads. I hope you have enjoyed reading it as much as I have enjoyed writing it. If nothing else, it should offer you an older and more traditional slant on the Tarot than you may currently use. So, if you keep my book on your shelf and consult it from time to time, the information that I have gathered here for you can only round out both your understanding of the cards and improve the quality of your readings.

Index